Magnetic
PUZZLE
PACK

by Ivan Moscovich

Sterling Publishing Co., Inc.
New York

10 9 8 7 6 5 4 3 2 1

Published by Sterling Publishing Co., Inc.
387 Park Avenue South, New York, NY 10016
© 2005 by Ivan Moscovich
Distributed in Canada by Sterling Publishing
c/o Canadian Manda Group, 165 Dufferin Street
Toronto, Ontario, Canada M6K 3H6
Distributed in Great Britain by Chrysalis Books Group PLC
The Chrysalis Building, Bramley Road, London W10 6SP, England
Distributed in Australia by Capricorn Link (Australia) Pty. Ltd.
P.O. Box 704, Windsor, NSW 2756, Australia

Printed in China

Sterling ISBN 1-4027-2576-0

For information about custom editions, special sales, premium and
corporate purchases, please contact Sterling Special Sales
Department at 800-805-5489 or specialsales@sterlingpub.com

Book design and layout by Judith Stagnitto Abbate / Abbate Design

CONTENTS

FOREWORD

To Anitta, Hila, and Emilia with love and dedication.

Games and puzzles have inspired people of all ages and in all parts of the world since the dawn of time. Riddles have entered mythology; puzzles have been discovered in prehistoric sites; board games like chess and checkers are found in civilizations the world over; and the principles of mathematics and logic are strongly built into their structures.

Games and the intellectual creativity they inspire are also perhaps the most important human form of leisure activity known to humans— recreation in the pure sense of the word. One of their charms is that they appeal to people from all walks of life.

But games and puzzles are not just for entertainment and fun. They are excellent educational tools for creative thinking and problem-solving. Even the simplest puzzles and games have subtle strategies and winning ways.

About This Book ...

Can you imagine having more than 90 games and puzzles to solve or play with your friends, all in a package you can carry in one hand?

This book is the equivalent of just that! It contains a selection of specially designed classic and original puzzles and games, complete with game boards, playing pieces, and instructions, for instant play in a car, train, airplane, at parties, or anywhere.

The diverse selection of puzzles and games represents a tribute to the puzzle pioneers Sam Loyd, Henry Dudeney, and many others, as well as to the modern puzzle and game creators with whom I have had the enormous privilege over more than 50 years to communicate, exchange ideas, collaborate, and create enjoyable friendships— to mention just a few: Martin Gardner, Sid Sackson, Claude Soucie, Mel Stover, Alex Randolph, Nob Yoshigahara, Edward Hordern, Jerry Slocum, Mark Setteducati, Dick Hess, Tim Rowett, Greg Frederickson, and many, many others.

—Ivan Moscovich

DIFFERENCE TRIANGLES

Two Triangular Number Puzzles

A set of consecutive numbers must be inserted in each triangular game board following two simple rules:

Each number may appear only once, and each number must be the difference of the two numbers immediately above it, as shown in the example.

PUZZLE 1

Numbers from 1 to 22, omitting number 15.

PUZZLE 2

Numbers from 1 to 33 omitting 16, 20, 22, 29, and 30.

Playing Pieces

1	2	3	4	5	6
7	8	9	10	11	12
13	14	15	16	17	18
19	20	21	22	23	24
25	26	27	28	31	32
33					

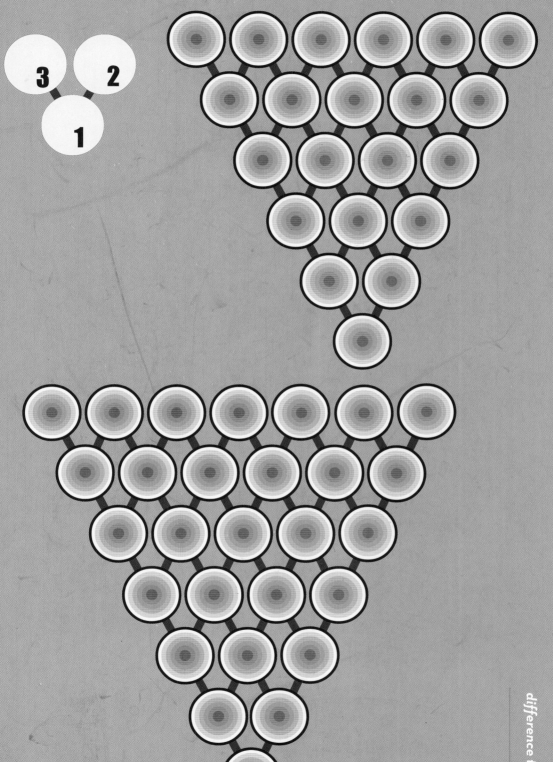

NUMBER CASCADES

Three Number Pattern Puzzles

Can you arrange the numbers from 1 to 4 (pictured), 1 to 9, 1 to 16, and 1 to 25, respectively, in the circles of the game boards, so that no circle has a circle with a higher value either next to it on the right or immediately below it?

Playing Pieces

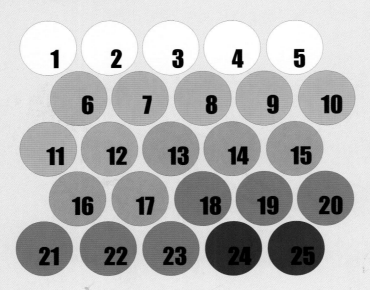

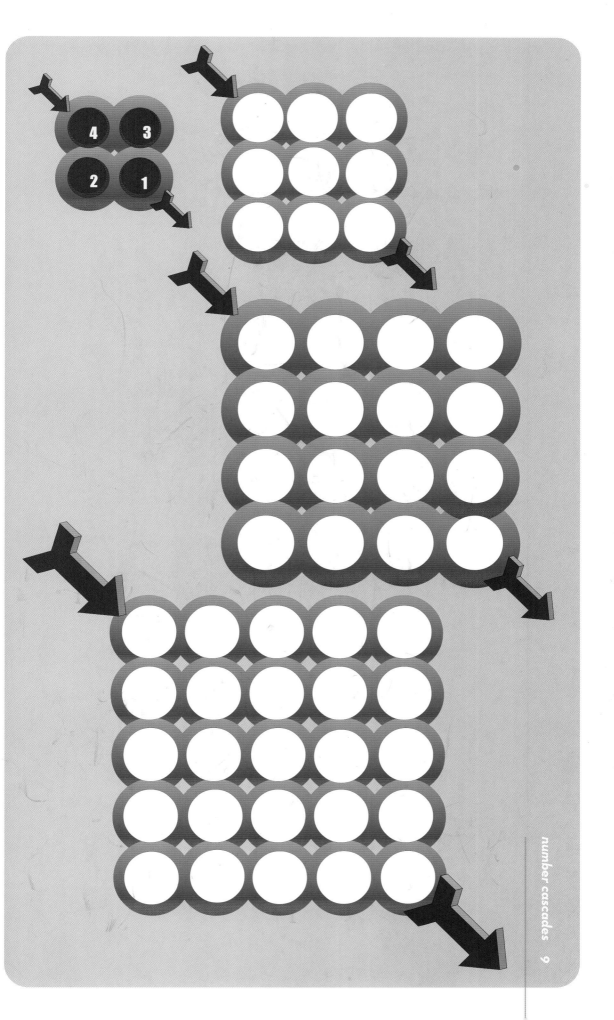

NO-TWO-IN-A-LINE HEXAGON

Can you place the seven playing pieces on the circles of the game board so that exactly one piece lies on any straight line in any direction?

Playing Pieces

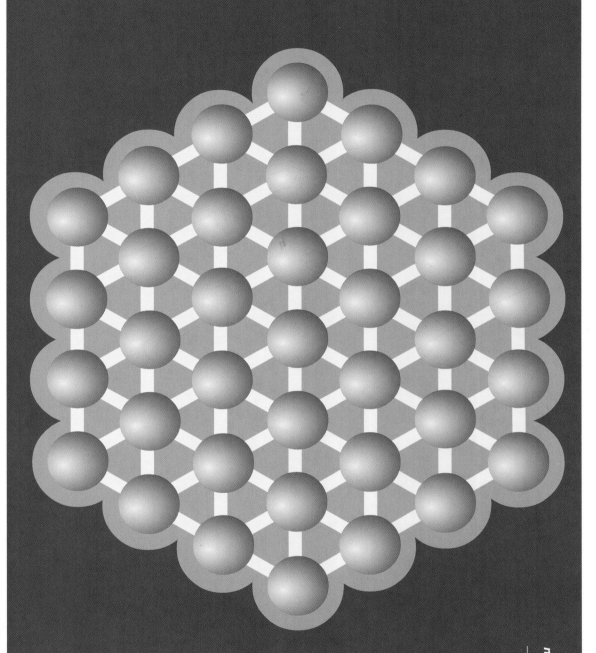

QUEENS' PROBLEMS

Queen's Increasing Tour Problem
The queen starts from the position shown, and has to execute a closed tour under the following conditions:

1. Each consecutive move has to be longer than the preceding one. Distance is measured in absolute terms, not by the number of squares: a move of one square horizontally or vertically is a distance of 1; a move of one square diagonally is a distance of $\sqrt{2}$.
2. The queen's moves may intersect, and she is also allowed to visit a square more than once.

A solution by Gilbert Obermair is shown below, in which the tour takes 12 moves having a total length of $24 + 24\sqrt{2} = 57.94$ units.

Playing Pieces

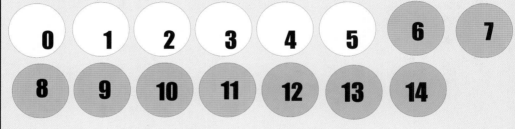

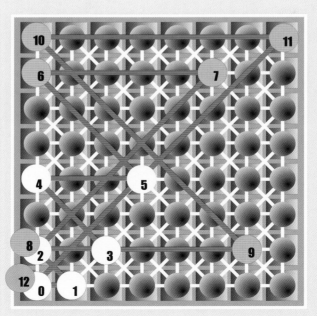

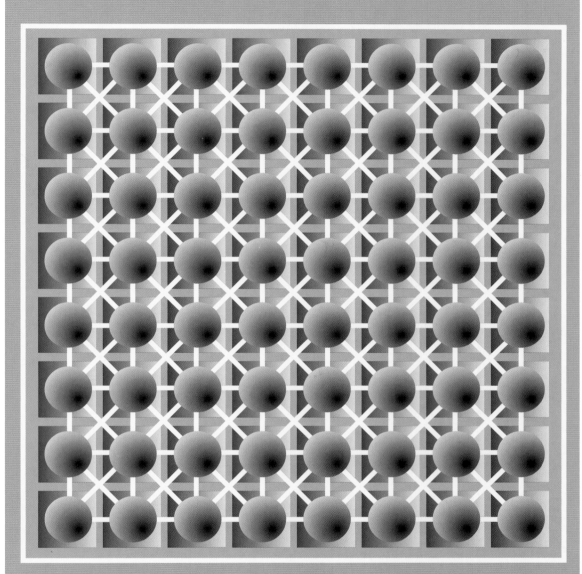

Queens' Placement Problems

Completely independent from the game of chess, problems associated with various chess pieces and their placements have entertained puzzlists for centuries.

The queen is by far the most powerful piece in chess, so it's no wonder some of the most challenging problems are associated with her. The following puzzles are some of the best problems in this category.

PUZZLE 1 *Queens' Domination* | What is the smallest number of chess queens that can be placed on the chessboard such that all squares are under attack:

1. Including the squares occupied by the queens themselves?
2. Excluding the squares occupied by the queens?

PUZZLE 2 *Queens' Standoff* | Can you place eight queens on the chessboard so that no queen is under attack by another? This problem was first posed in 1848 by Max Bezzel. There are 12 essentially different solutions. How many of them can you find?

PUZZLE 3 *Queens' Color Standoff 1* | Can you place three orange queens, three blue queens, and four green queens on a chessboard so that no queen of one color is attacked by a queen of another color?

PUZZLE 4 *Queens' Color Standoff 2* | Can you place nine red queens (use pink and orange markers) and ten blue queens (use blue and green markers) on a chessboard so that no queen of one color set is attacked by a queen of another color set?

PUZZLE 5 *Queens' Color Standoff 3* | Can you place four orange queens, five blue queens, and six green queens on a chessboard so that no queen of one color is attacked by a queen of another color?

PUZZLE 6 *Queens' Color Standoff 4* | Can you place three pink queens, three blue queens, three green queens, and three yellow queens on a chessboard so that no queen of one color is attacked by a queen of another color?

Playing Pieces

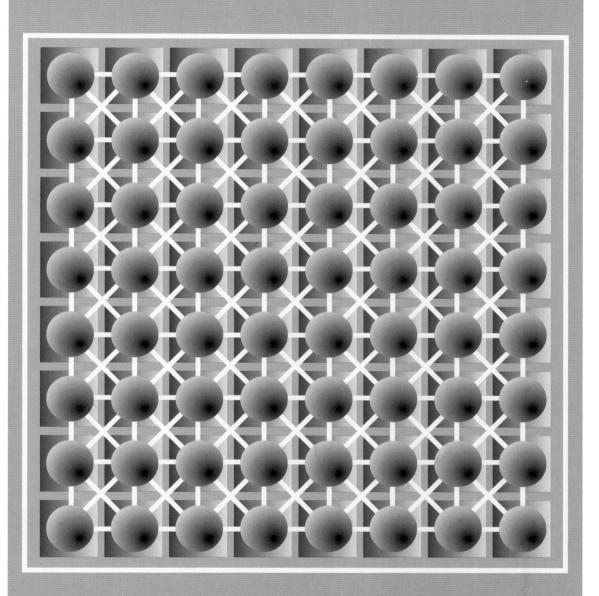

PACKING SQUARES

Two Packing Puzzles

What is the smallest size that a large square can be when fit with *n* unit squares into it without overlap?

If the squares are not allowed to tilt, the problem is quite easy. The problem is more challenging when the squares are allowed to tilt in any orientation, as is allowed in our puzzles.

PUZZLE 1 *Packing 18 Unit Squares* | Eighteen identical unit squares have to be packed into the yellow square area. There are two rules for packing:

1. No parts of the 18 unit squares are allowed to trespass onto the orange surrounding area.
2. No overlapping of the squares is allowed.

PUZZLE 2 *Packing 26 Unit Squares* | Twenty-six unit squares have to be packed into the yellow square area. The rules of packing from Puzzle 1 still apply.

Playing Pieces

n=1; k=1

n=2; k=2   n=3; k=2   n=4; k=2

n=5; k=2.707

n=6; k=3   n=7; k=3

n=8; k=3   n=9; k=3

n=10; k=3.707   n=10; k=3.707

Packing Unit Squares | Best results known for packing *n* unit squares into the smallest squares possible, when *n* ranges from 1 to 10, and *k* indicates the length of the side of the large square.

Puzzle 1: 18 squares

Puzzle 2: 26 squares

BUSY BEES

PUZZLE

The object is to cover the board with the 16 colored hexagons, one by one, according to the following rules:

1. Do not place a piece on a hexagon of the same color, or horizontally, vertically, or diagonally adjacent to a hexagon of the same color.
2. After each turn, a hexagon on the board assumes the color of the hexagon that covers it, as far as rule 1 is concerned on subsequent moves.
3. A piece may not be played on top of another piece.
4. The game board must be fully covered by the hexagons after the last move.

GAME

One or more players take turns by placing the 16 colored tiles on the game board according to the above rules.

The first player unable to place a hexagon is the loser.

Playing Pieces

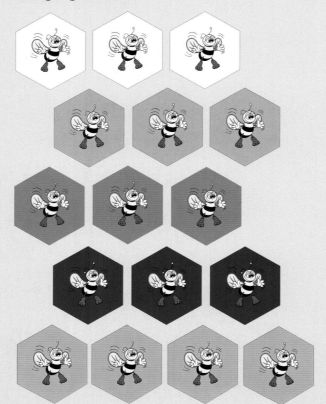

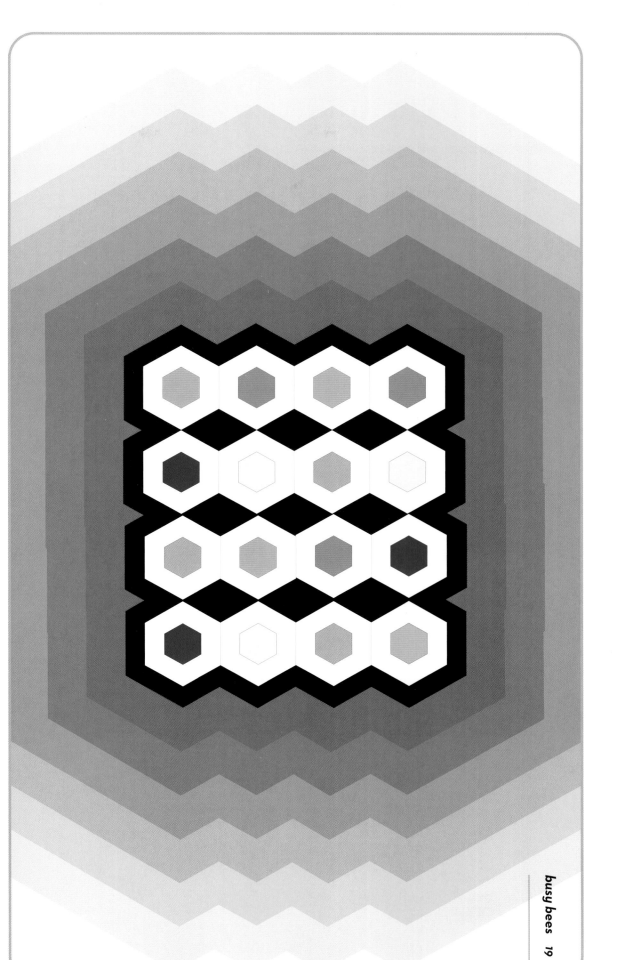

HYPERCUBE

Fit the numbers from 0 to 15 in the circles of the "hypercube" so that the numbers on the corners of each of the eight skeleton cubes add up to 60.

A hypercube is a four-dimensional cube, shown here in a two-dimensional approximation.

Confined as we are to three dimensions, it is difficult for our brains to visualize four-dimensional space, but mathematical training can help develop such an ability.

Playing Pieces

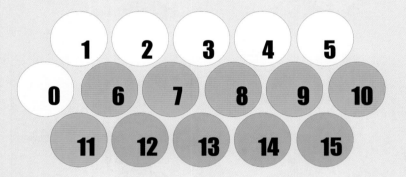

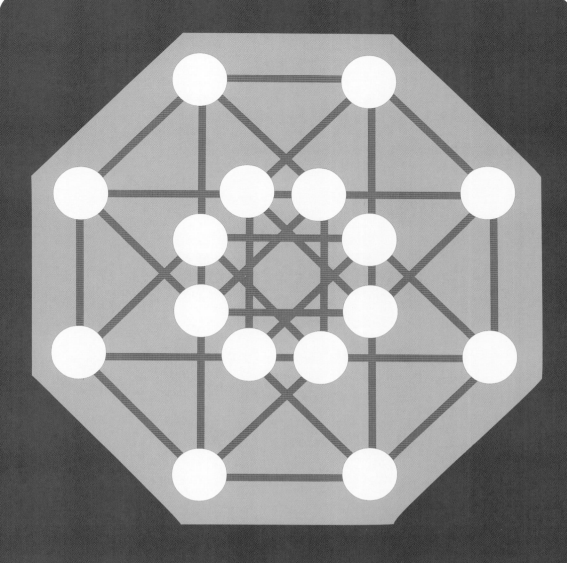

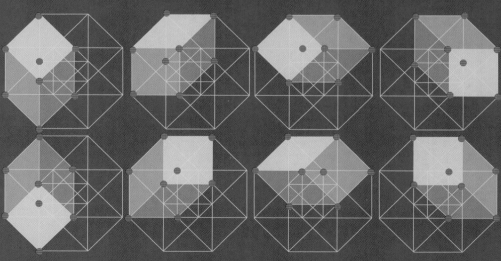

GRAECO-LATIN MAGIC SQUARES

Graeco-Latin Magic Color Square of Order 4

PUZZLE

Can you distribute the sets of color squares in the game boards, according to the rules of Graeco-Latin squares?

Each square consists of two Latin squares of order 4 (one of circle pieces, the other of square pieces) that have been super-imposed so that each cell contains one element of each square, each element of one square is combined with an element of the second square only once, and each row and column contains every element from both squares.

GAME

A challenging and addictive competition game can be played between two or more players according to these simple rules:

Players take turns placing a randomly selected tile (or one of an evenly divided set of tiles for each player) adjacent to a previously placed tile anywhere on the board, according to the above described rules of Graeco-Latin squares.

The winner is the last player able to make a valid move. Or, if so decided, the winner can be the player who first creates a valid row or column.

Playing Pieces

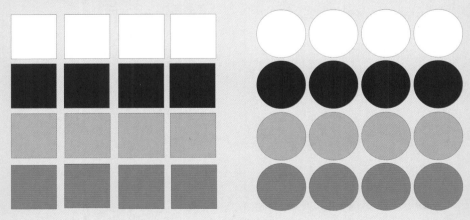

Near the end of his life, the great mathematician Leonhard Euler devised new types of magic squares, the Latin square and the Graeco-Latin square.

Latin and Graeco-Latin magic squares are not mere diversions—they have valuable applications in experimental science.

Suppose an agricultural researcher wished to test the effect of seven types of fungicides on wheat plants. He might divide an experimental field into seven parallel strips and treat each strip with a different fungicide. But such a test might be biased because of a favorable field condition in one of the plots—say, in the easternmost or southernmost strip. The best way to control for such biases is to divide the field into 49 plots in a seven-by-seven matrix and apply the chemicals according to the prescriptions of a Latin square. That way each fungicide is tested in every field condition. If the experiment needed to test the seven fungicides on seven different strains of wheat, then a Graeco-Latin square could be applied.

In this way, Euler's recreational problem has become a widely useful design, not only in agriculture, but also in biology, sociology, medicine, and even marketing. The "cell" need not, of course, be a piece of land. It might be a cow, a patient, a leaf, a cage of animals, a city, a period of time, and so on. The square is simply a way to combine variable elements in unique ways.

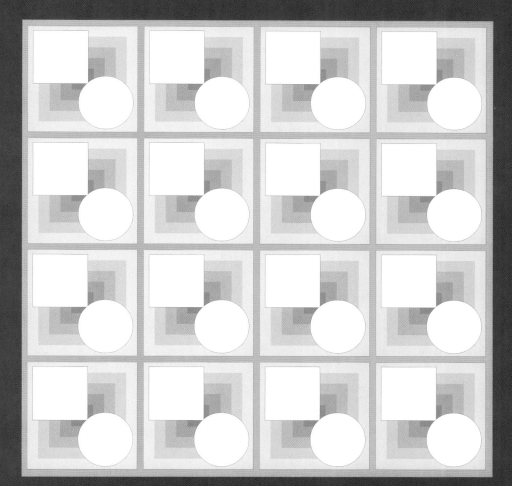

Graeco-Latin Magic Color Square of Order 5

PUZZLE

Can you distribute the sets of color circles and squares in the game board, according to the rules of Graeco-Latin squares? The square consists of two Latin squares of order 5 (one of circular pieces, the other of square pieces) that have been superimposed so that each cell contains one element of each square, each element of one square is combined with an element of the second square only once, and each row and column contains every element from both squares.

GAME

A challenging and addictive competition game can be played between two or more players according to these simple rules:

Players take turns placing a randomly selected tile (or one of an evenly divided set of tiles for each player) adjacent to a previously placed tile anywhere on the board, according to the above described rules of Graeco-Latin squares.

The winner is the last player able to make a valid move. Or, if so decided, the winner can be the player who first creates a valid row or column.

Playing Pieces

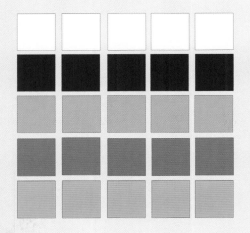 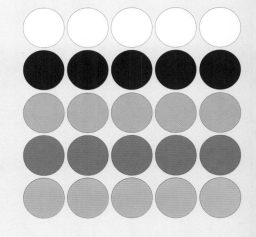

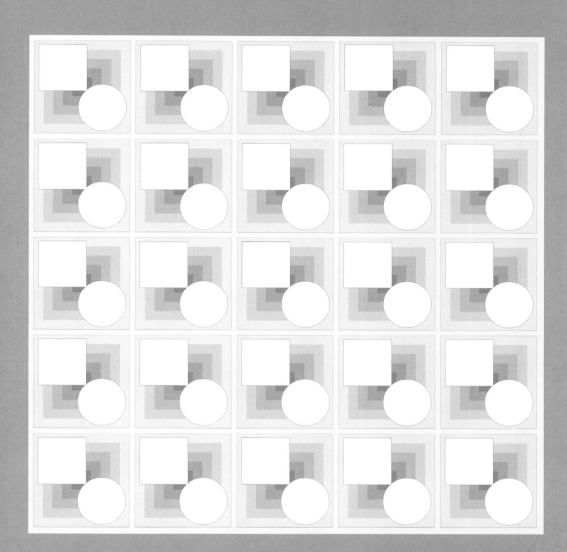

BRAX

A Two-Player Game

This classic was developed a hundred years ago in New York.

Each player starts with five pieces initially arranged as shown. The object is to capture the opponent's pieces, according to the following rules:

1. A move consists of sliding a piece up two spaces along a line of the player's color, or one space along a line of the opponent's color. When moving two spaces, a piece may change directions in the middle of the move, so long as it stays on the same color line.
2. A piece is captured and removed when an opposing piece lands on top of it.
3. Jumping over other pieces is not permitted.

Playing Pieces

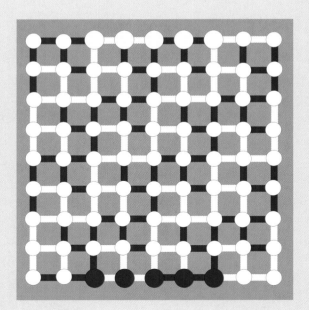

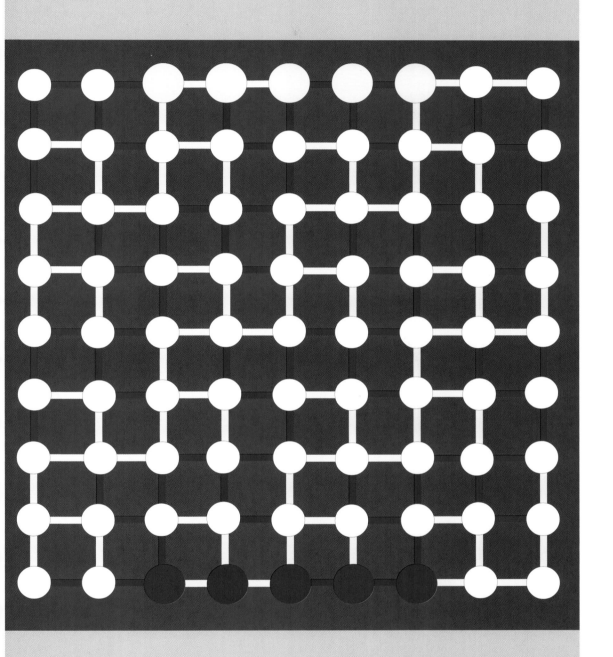

ARROW NUMBER PUZZLES

Place sixteen arrows in the 4-by-4 game board in any of the eight possible orientations so that the number of arrows pointing to each number on the periphery will match that number.

As an example, we've provided a solved puzzle below. Multiple solutions may be possible.

Playing Pieces

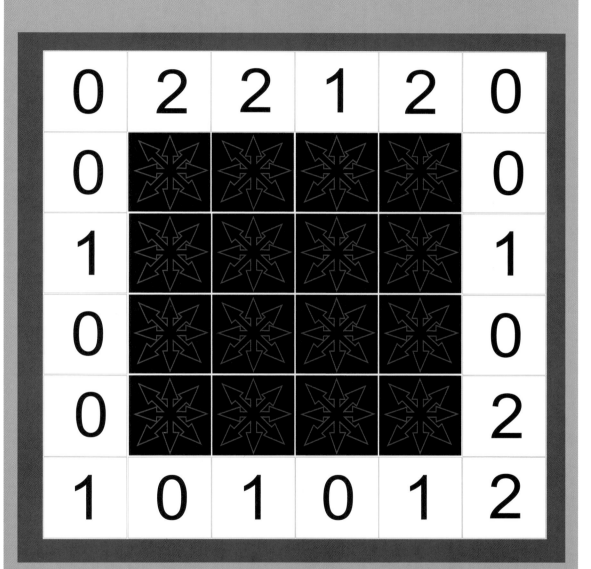

Arrow Number Puzzles

PUZZLE 2

Follow the instructions on page 28. As an example, there is a sample puzzle below. Multiple solutions may be possible.

Playing Pieces

2	2	0	0	0	2
1	↖	←	→	↗	1
0	↑	↙	↗	↓	0
0	↑	↘	↘	↓	0
1	↙	←	→	↘	1
2	0	0	0	2	2

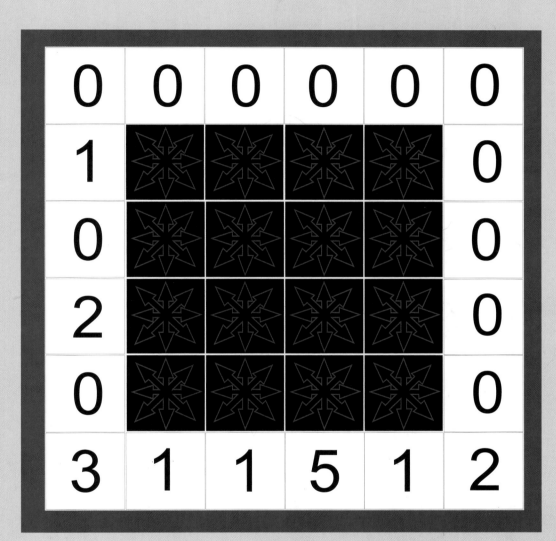

0	0	0	0	0	0
1					0
0					0
2					0
0					0
3	1	1	5	1	2

Arrow Number Puzzles

PUZZLE 3

Follow the instructions on page 28. As an example, there is a sample puzzle below. Multiple solutions may be possible.

Playing Pieces

	2	2	0	0	0	2	
1							1
0							0
0							0
1							1
	2	0	0	0	2	2	

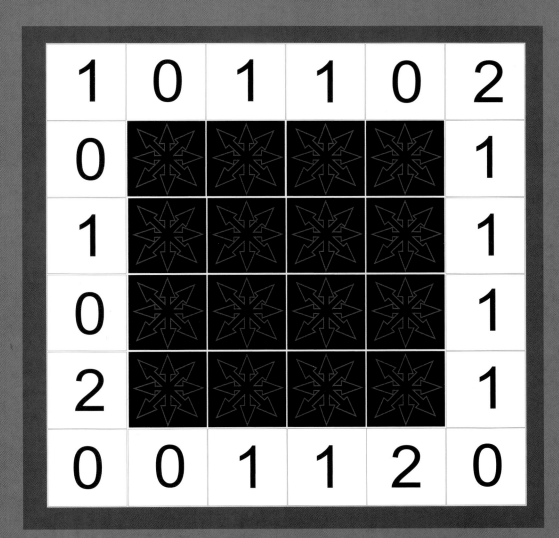

MAGIC HEXAGRAMS

Two Number Puzzles

MAGIC HEXAGRAM 1

Can you place the numbers from 1 to 12 in the circles of the small six-pointed star so that the numbers in each straight line add up to 26?

MAGIC HEXAGRAM 2

Can you place the numbers from 1 to 19 in the circles of the large six-pointed star so that the numbers in each line add up to 46?

Playing Pieces

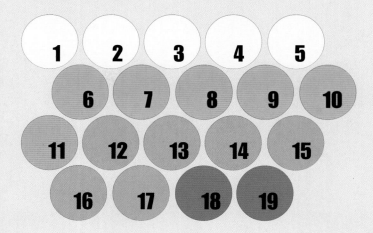

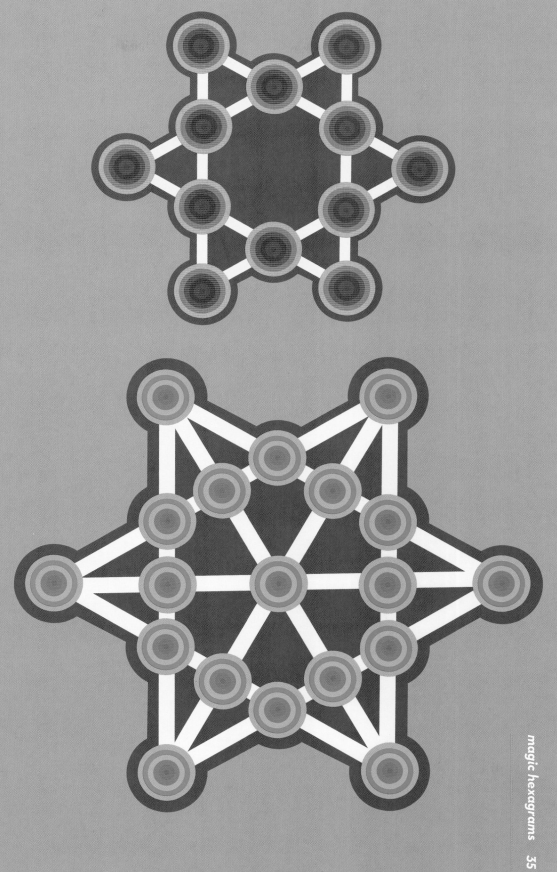

EIGHT-BLOCK SLIDING PUZZLE

The numbers from 8 to 1 are distributed in the 3-by-3 game board as shown with one field left empty in the initial configuration (below left).

The object of the puzzle is to rearrange the tiles in a consecutive order from 1 to 8 by sliding the blocks into the end configuration shown below on the right.

What is the minimum number of moves necessary to achieve the transformation?

Playing Pieces

| 1 | 2 | 3 | 4 | 5 | 6 | 7 | 8 |

Sliding Block Puzzles

Sliding block puzzles have teased the minds of children and adults alike for more than a hundred years. There is a peculiar fascination of pushing pieces around a board to reach a particular position or achieve a certain objective. Once picked up and started, people find them hard to put down. Many sliding block puzzles are very easy to solve, but some can be very difficult.

The fascination does not stop at merely finding a solution. There is a much greater satisfaction in finding the minimum number of moves to reach the solution, or in the case of harder puzzles, a shorter solution than was known before.

No one seems to know when the first sliding block puzzle was invented or produced. What is certain is that Sam Loyd made them famous more than a hundred years ago in the 1870's with his still well-known and produced 14-15 puzzle. He probably did, however, take the idea for this puzzle from an older French puzzle-game called Le Jeu de Taquain.

After Sam Loyd's 14-15 puzzle, many variations of this puzzle came onto the market. It was not until 1909 that a puzzle was patented, known under hundreds of names.

SPIDERWEB

A Two-Player Board Game

Two players place their sets of four pieces on the board as indicated. They alternate moves with the objective being to block the opponent's pieces so that they cannot move.

A move may be:

1. From one of the outer circles to an adjacent empty circle.
2. From one of the outer circles to the center, provided that the outer circle is adjacent to at least one of the opponent's pieces.
3. From the center to an outside circle.

Playing Pieces

BISHOPS' EXCHANGE

Four yellow and four orange bishops are placed on a 4-by-5 game board as shown.

What is the minimum number of moves needed to exchange the two sets of pieces?

Playing Pieces

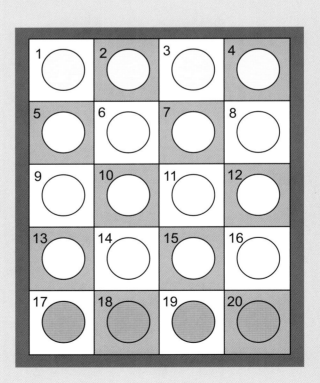

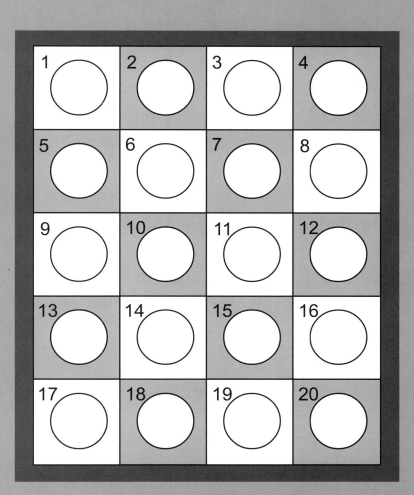

ARROW
TOURS 1

Fourteen arrows are distributed in the 7-by-7 game board as shown. Leaving the arrows on the same squares, reorient them in one of the eight possible directions to form a continuous closed loop of straight lines in the directions indicated by the arrows and without any lines crossing.

What is the greatest number of squares you can visit with the lines?

Playing Pieces

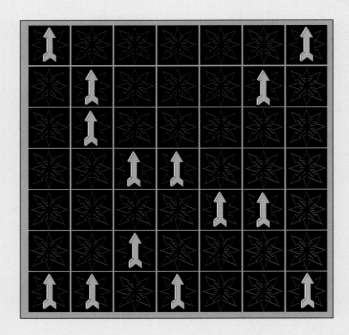

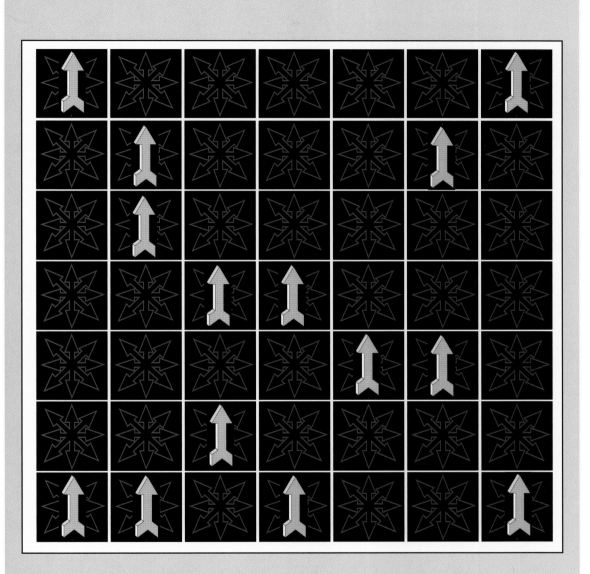

ARROW TOURS 2

Fourteen arrows are distributed in the 8-by-8 game board as shown below.

Leaving the arrows on the same squares as they start on, reorient them in one of the eight possible directions to form a continuous loop of straight lines in the directions indicated by the arrows.

In this puzzle, lines may intersect and pass through squares more than once.

Can you visit all 64 squares on the game board?

Playing Pieces

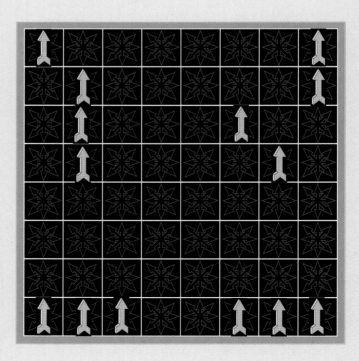

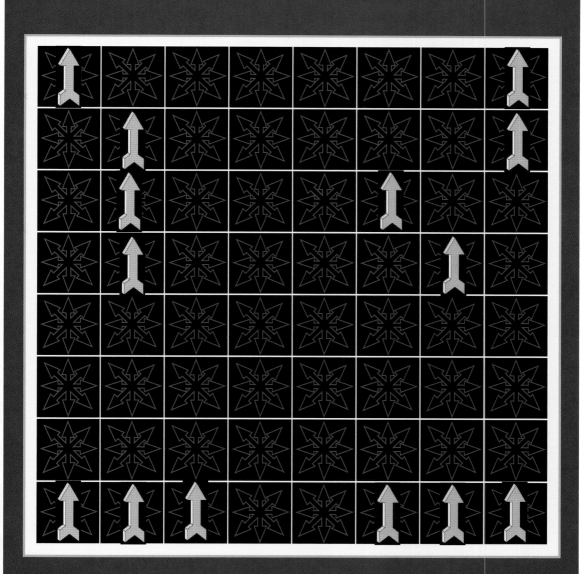

HONEYCOMBS

The Four-Color Theorem Puzzle-Game

PUZZLE

Arrange the set of 16 hexagons on the game board so that no adjacent hexagons are the same color.

GAME

The 16 hexagons are shuffled face down. Players take turns choosing a hexagon and placing it on the game board adjacent to a hexagon already placed. No adjacent hexagons can be of the same color.

A player who cannot place a hexagon loses his turn. The player who manages to make the last legal move is the winner.

Playing Pieces

The Four-Color Theorem

Until recently this theorem was known as the Four-Color Problem: simple enough to state, but not so easy to prove.

How many colors are needed so that any map can be colored in such a way that no adjacent regions (which must touch along an edge, not just at a point) have the same color?

It is not hard to show that at least four colors are needed. In the 19th century a mathematician named Kemper published a proof that no map needed five colors. Ten years later it was noticed that he had made a subtle but crucial mistake, and that his proof showed that no map required six colors. Ever since, that has left a tantalizing gap for mathematicians.

For about a hundred years people wrestled with the problem. Nobody could find a map that actually needed five colors, but nobody could show conclusively that no such map existed either. It became famous as one of the simplest remaining unsolved classical mathematical problems. To make matters worse, analogous problems dealing with more complicated surfaces could always be answered conclusively. For example, a map on a doughnut can always be colored with seven colors, and there exist maps for which six colors do the job. On a strange one-sided surface called a Klein bottle, six colors are both necessary and sufficient.

Then in the late 1970s, two mathematicians at the University of Illinois solved the problem, and so now we have the Four-Color Theorem, on which our game is based.

Q-BITS

There are many different ways to arrange the 16 tiles shown below in a 4-by-4 game board. But is it possible to do this in such a way that the colors of adjacent tiles match on all edges? Try it!

How many different solutions can you find? See who can discover the most different solutions in a given time.

GAME

The tiles are mixed facedown. In turn, each player takes a tile and places it on the board to fit exactly to one of the sides of an already placed playing piece on the game board, with touching colors matching. On the first turn, you do not need to match the tile to an already placed playing piece.

The first player unable to place a tile on his turn is the loser. The longest game can go on for 16 moves. What is the shortest possible game, or what is the smallest number of tiles one can place on the board so as to block it completely, making any further placing of tiles impossible?

Playing Pieces

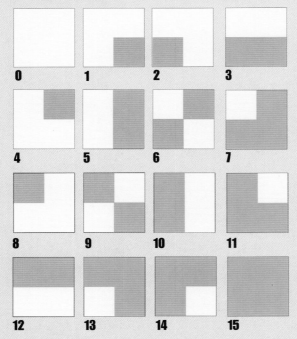

The playing pieces for the Q-Bits game represent the first 16 numbers in the binary number system, starting with zero as shown.

Under scrutiny you may notice that there are altogether only six basically different tiles, some of which, in different orientations, have different binary numerical values (a possible scoring system for game results). Try making up your own game variations using this scoring system.

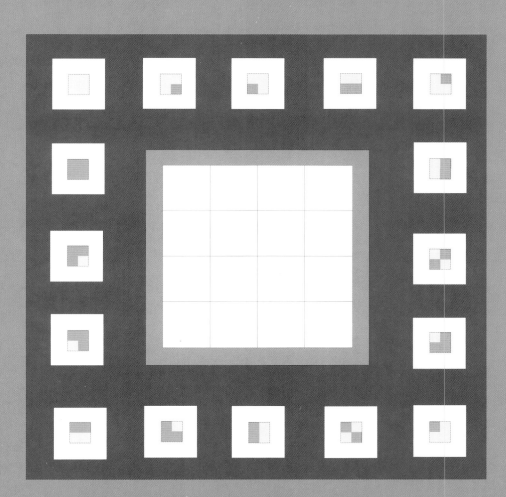

NO-THREE-IN-A-LINE

Can you place 16 counters on the game board so that no three counters will lie on any straight line (horizontally, vertically, or diagonally)?

The first two counters have already been placed as shown.

Playing Pieces

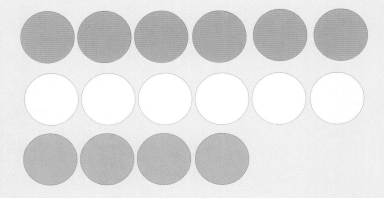

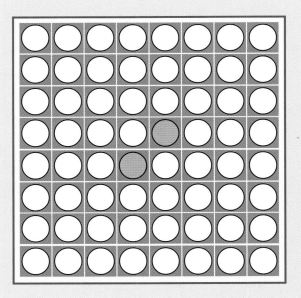

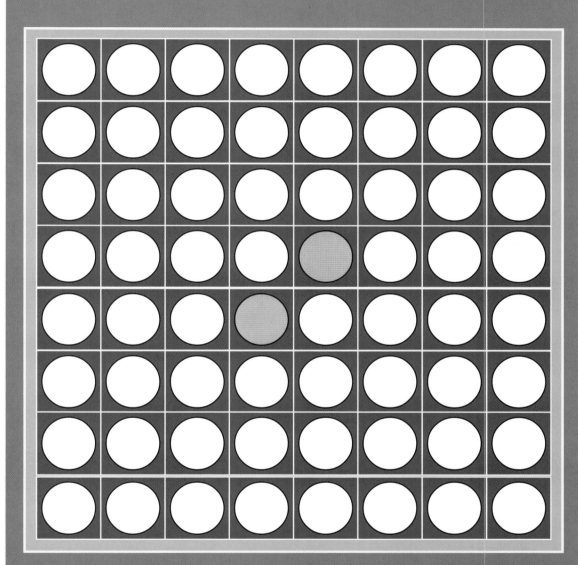

HEX CHECKERS

Many three-player checkers variants have been designed, some dating to Victorian times.

Our game is a simple variation of the idea. The three players each have six playing pieces at the initial positions shown.

Jumps and multiple jumps are as in standard checkers. Pieces move along straight lines, and each player is allowed to capture pieces from either opponent or both opponents. The game ends when one of the players eliminates his two opponents or leaves their remaining pieces such that they have no legal move.

Pieces moved from their bases may not return to any hexagon of the same colored base during a game, except at the end of jumps. They may also pass through such hexagons as part of a multiple jump.

Playing Pieces

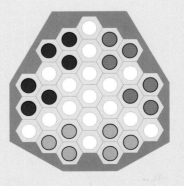

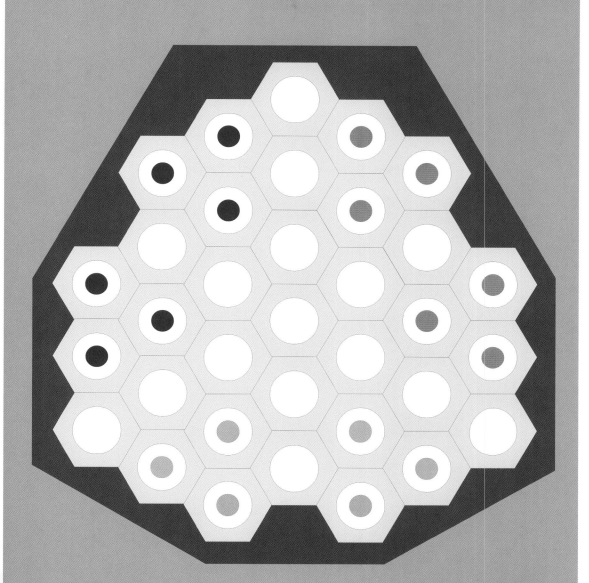

MATCHSTICK PUZZLES

PUZZLE 1

Sixteen matchsticks form four identical squares. Using the same number of matchsticks can you form five squares of the same size?

PUZZLE 2

Take away five matchsticks to leave five identical triangles.

PUZZLE 3

Change the position of six matchsticks to form a house.

Playing Pieces

create 5 squares

create 3 squares

create 2 squares

move 2 matches

create 5 squares

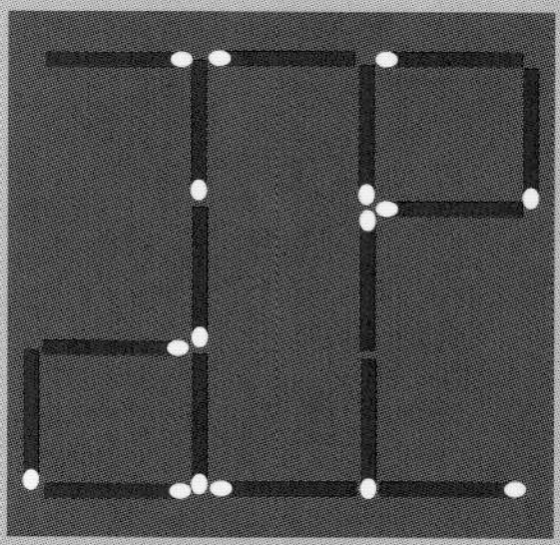

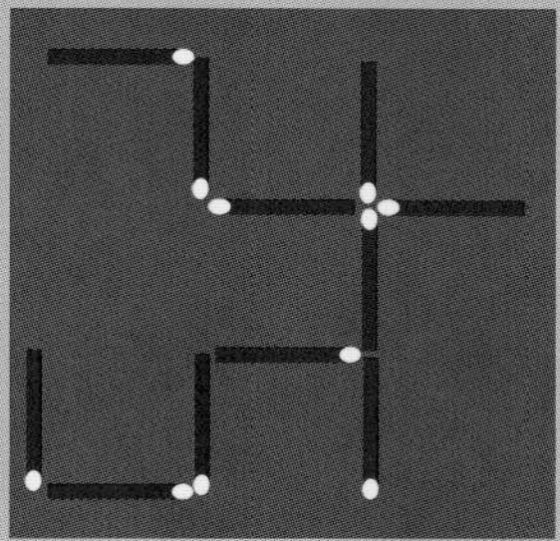

create 3 squares

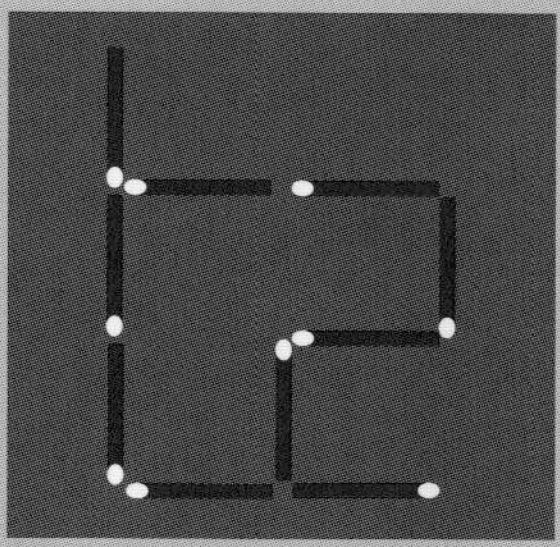

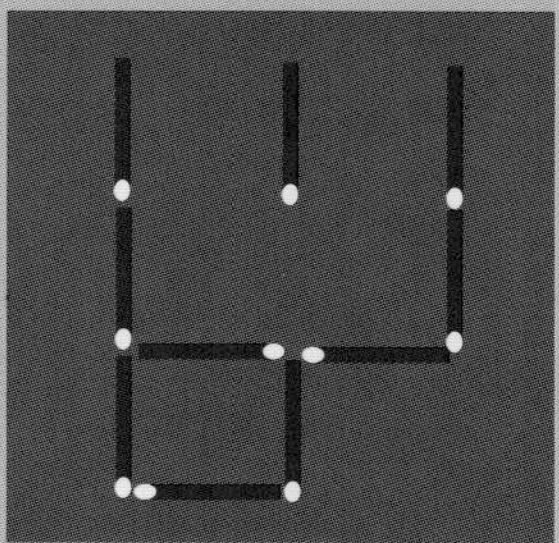

create 2 squares

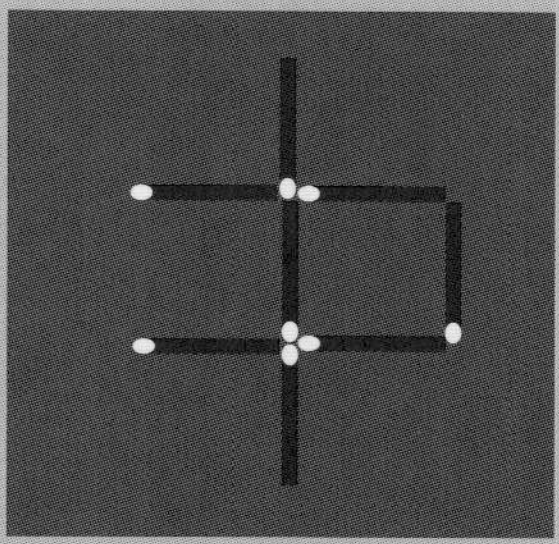

move 3 matches

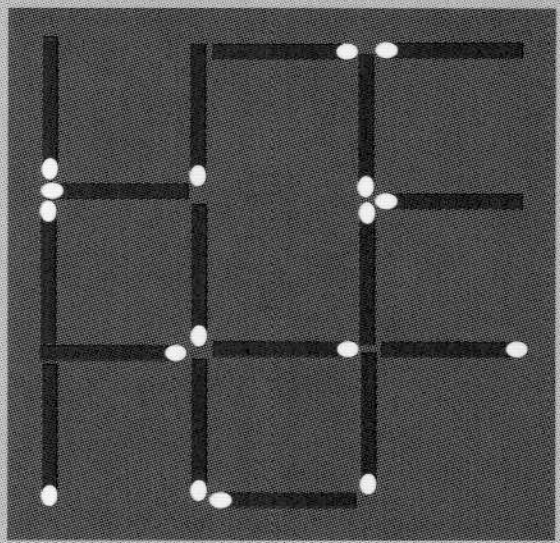

TRICKY DISCS PUZZLE

A Classic Sliding Disc Puzzle

Two sets of five playing pieces are placed as shown below: five orange pieces on the left, five blue pieces on the right, with one empty space between them.

The object of the puzzle is to reverse the placement of the two sets as shown on the game board, carefully observing the following rules:

1. Only one disc can be moved at a time.
2. A disc can move into an adjacent empty space.
3. A disc can jump over one of the opposite colors into a space immediately beyond it.
4. A disc may not jump over another of its own color.
5. Orange discs may only move to the right and blue discs may only move to the left.

What is the minimum number of moves to solve the puzzle? Can you find an algorithm which would give the number of moves for two sets of any number of discs (for example, two sets of 10 discs each)?

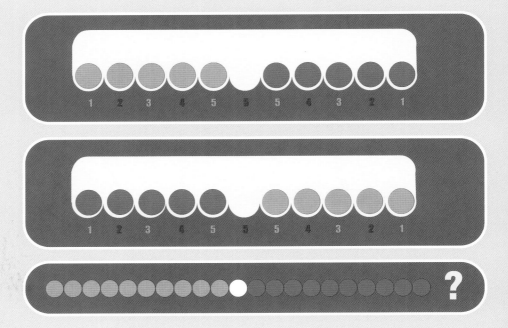

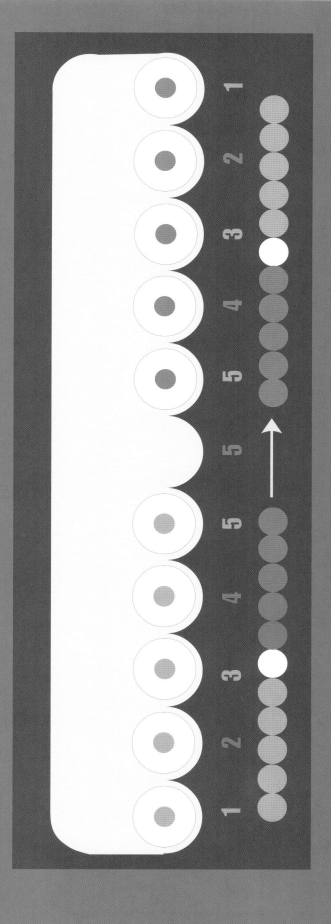

BATTLEFIELD

Two-Player Board Game

Each player has 10 pieces in two colors, placed in the initial configurations as indicated below.

Rules

1. The object of both players is to get as many pieces as possible to the home of the opponent.
2. On unfortified squares, the moves are the same as for pawns in chess: one square at a time forward, or one square diagonally when capturing an opponent's piece, which is then removed.
3. When standing on one's own fortification, moves and captures can be made both forward and diagonally.
4. When standing on the enemy's fortification, a piece cannot capture but can be captured.
5. After passing the enemy's fortification, the pieces again capture normally.
6. No sideways or backward moves are allowed.
7. There is no obligation to capture at any stage of the game.

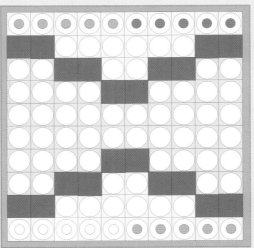

Home—Player 2

Fortification—Player 2

Battlefield

Fortification—Player 1

Home—Player 1

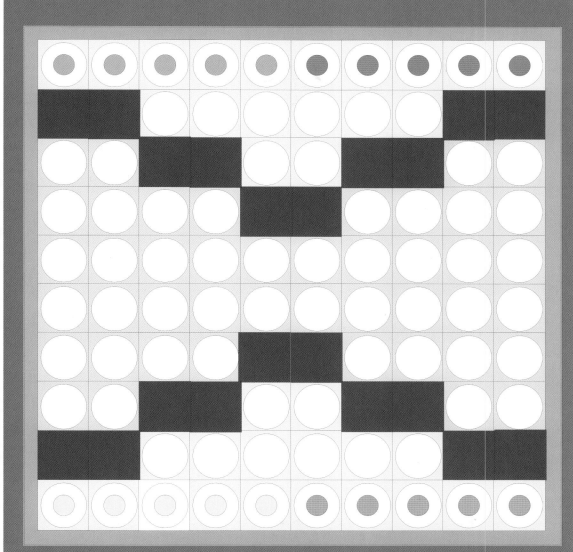

SNEAKY SLIDES

You need eight consecutively numbered playing pieces as shown below.

The object of the puzzle is to place the eight pieces in succession on eight circles of the game board, according to the following simple rule:

Every piece must be first placed on an empty circle of the game board and from there slid along one of the connected lines to an adjacent empty circle where it will remain until the end of the game.

There is a simple strategy to complete the puzzle every time, no matter where you start. Can you work it out?

Playing Pieces

1 2 3 4 5 6 7 8

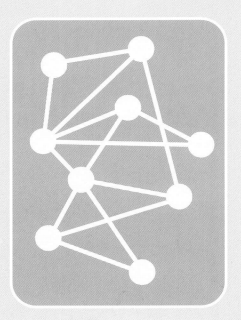

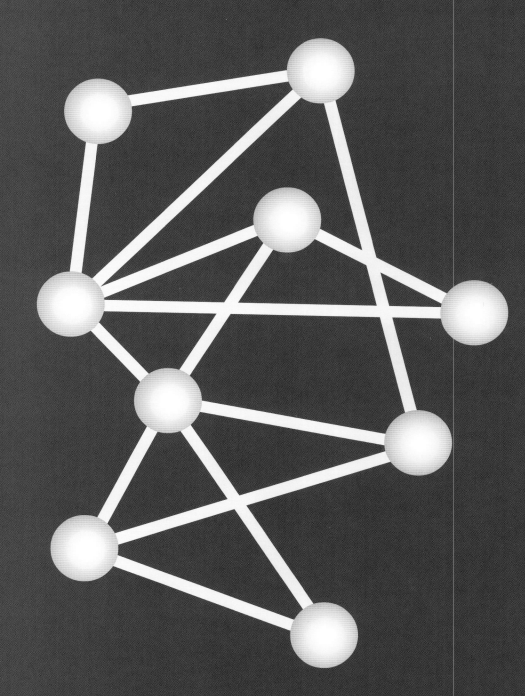

CHARLIE

A Two-Player Game

Two players each have nine pieces in three colors (one player round, the other square) with the initial placement on the board as shown.

The object of both players is to transfer their pieces to the opposite starting line on the correct colors.

Rules:
1. A piece can move forward, backward, sideways, or diagonally to an adjoining square of the same color.
2. Jumps are allowed in the same directions over pieces of all colors.
3. As in checkers, multiple jumps are allowed with changes of direction between jumps. The only condition is that a piece must finish the multiple jump on a square of its own color. The intermediate jumps may land on squares of any color.
4. No pieces are removed from the game board after a jump.

Playing Pieces

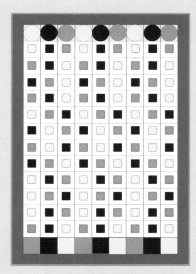

ARROW-MINDED GAME

Competition Game

GAME 1

Any number of players can compete.

One of the players distributes the 15 arrows along the 15 lines, one arrow on each line, oriented in one of the two possible directions on each line. This should be done out of the view of the other players.

The next player then has to distribute his 19 numbered pieces to create a continuous number path from 1 to 19, from intersection to intersection, visiting each intersection only once, and moving on each line in the direction of the arrow on that line. Skipping intersections is not allowed.

Start at any intersection with the 1 piece. You can change your path to another line at any intersection.

You may wish to set a time limit for scoring (say, five minutes, or less) once you are more familiar with the game. A player's score is the number of pieces played within the time limit, plus a 10-point bonus if all 19 pieces are placed.

GAME 2

Two-person competition game.

The arrows are randomly distributed on the board. Players take turns placing number pieces according to the rules above. The first player unable to make a legal move is the loser.

It should be noted that with a random placement of the arrows, it is not always possible to place the complete set of pieces.

Playing Pieces

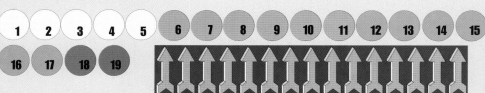

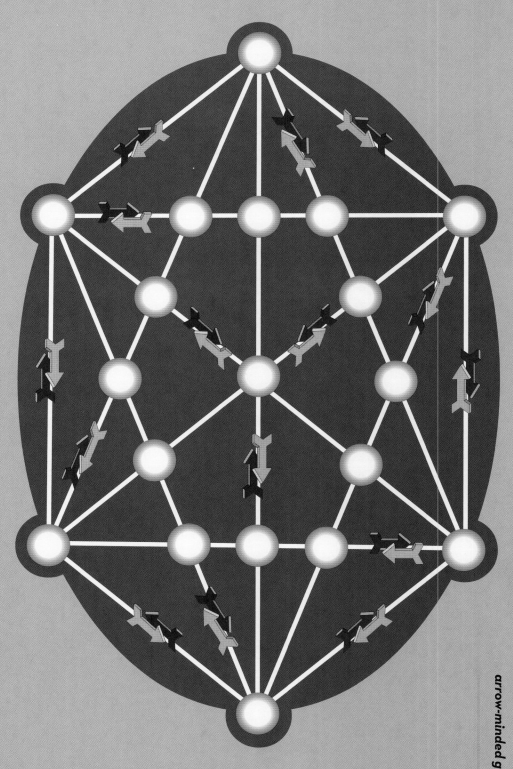

MAGIC WHEELS

Distribute the numbers from 1 to 12 on the intersections of four circles so that the six numbers on each circle add up to 39.

Playing Pieces

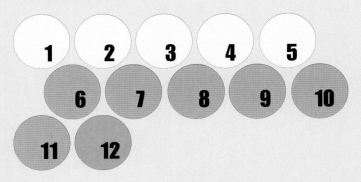

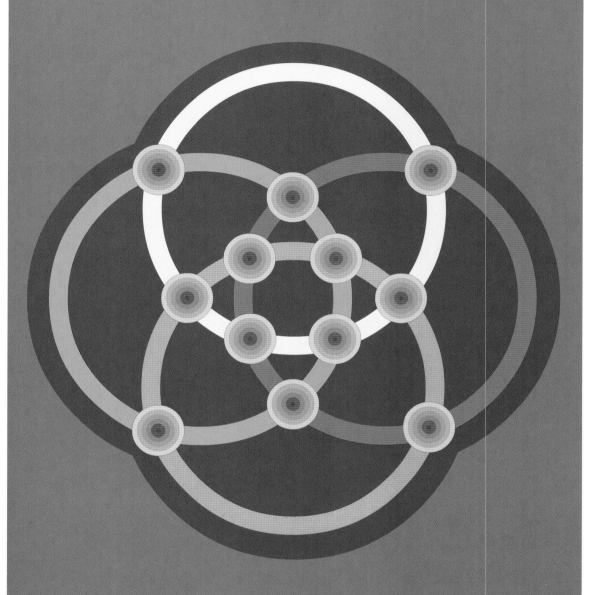

JOURNEY AROUND A DODECAHEDRON

The Icosian Game of Hamilton

So far we have been traversing graphs on the plane. A more difficult group of problems involves finding routes on three-dimensional objects.

One of the first (and now a classic) was invented by W.R. Hamilton in 1859, involving a dodecahedron.

He asked whether a route along the edges exists which would come back to the starting point after visiting all 20 vertices and without retracing an edge. (Note: In a Hamiltonian path or circuit, all the vertices must be visited, while some of the edges can be left out.)

To make it easier to solve such problems, Hamilton used a two-dimensional diagram of the dodecahedron (a so-called Schlegel diagram), which is topologically equivalent to the three-dimensional solid.

Hamilton devised a branch of mathematics to solve similar path-tracing problems on three-dimensional solids, called *Icosian calculus*.

Playing Pieces

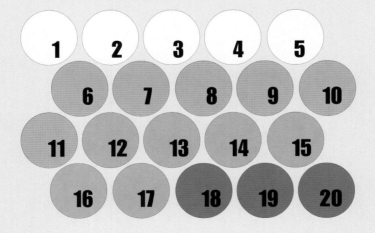

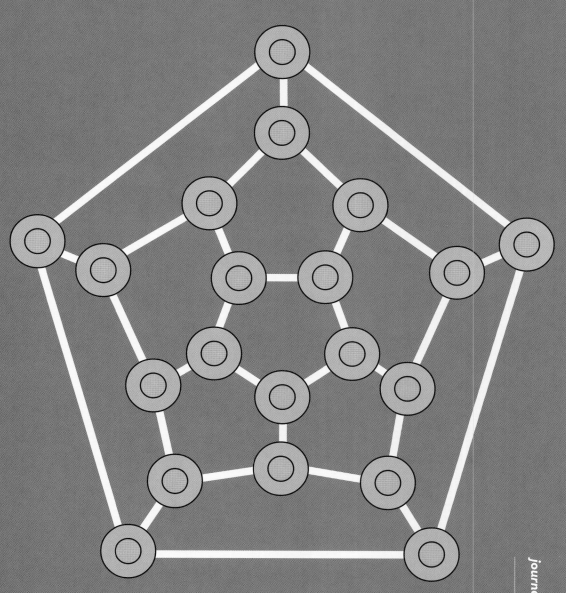

ARROW-MINDED PUZZLE 1

See page 64 for the rules to the Arrow-Minded Game. Can you place all 19 pieces on this board according to the rules?

Playing Pieces

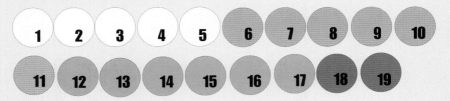

Record your solution

Mathematical background on Arrow-Minded Puzzles

The Arrow-Minded Puzzle was inspired by the famous Icosian Game of Hamilton. Its design offers 32,786 different game situations, each one a different puzzle to solve. You can play and solve a different Arrow-Minded Puzzle for the next 10 years.

Out of all the possibilities, 27,846 puzzles have complete solutions of which 190 solutions are cyclic (closed paths returning to point 1).

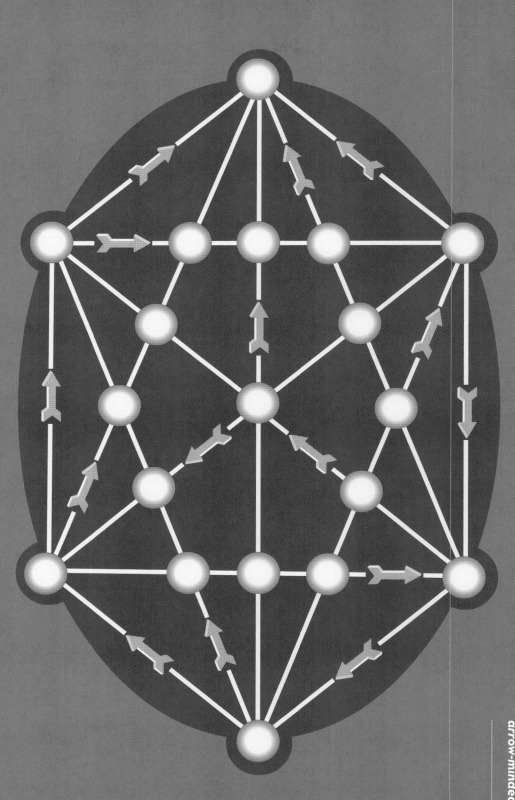

ARROW-MINDED PUZZLE 2

See page 64 for the rules to the Arrow-Minded Game. Can you place all 19 pieces on this board according to the rules?

Playing Pieces

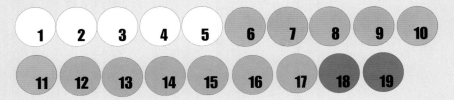

Record your solution

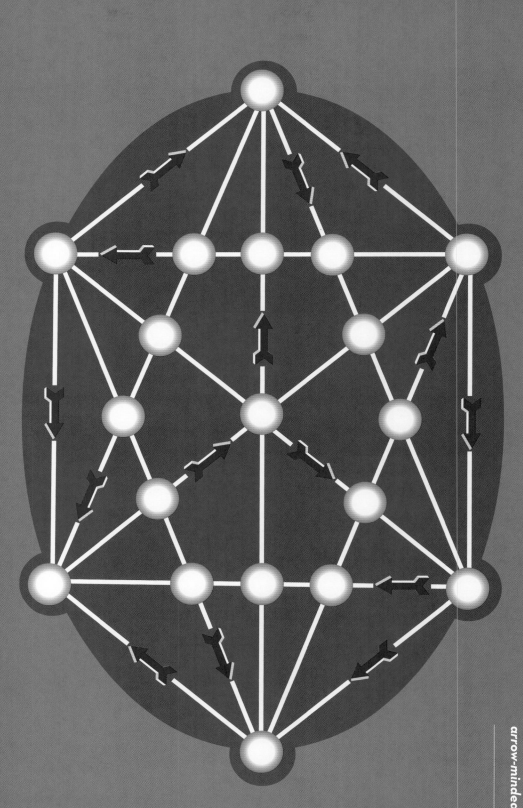

ARROW-MINDED PUZZLE 3

See page 64 for the rules to the Arrow-Minded Game. Can you place all 19 pieces on this board according to the rules?

Playing Pieces

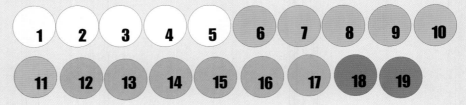

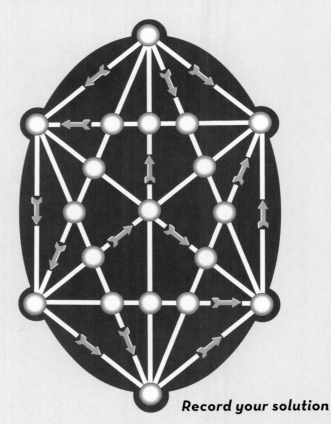

Record your solution

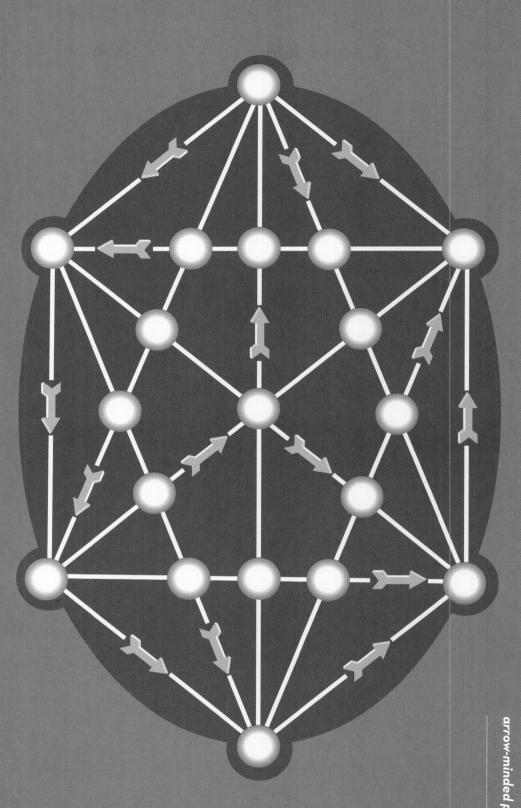

LINES IN THE SKY

Use the colored sticks to travel from the red star at the top of the page to the red star at the bottom. Sticks may only be placed so that they precisely overlap a star at each end. Not all pieces need to be used.

Playing Pieces

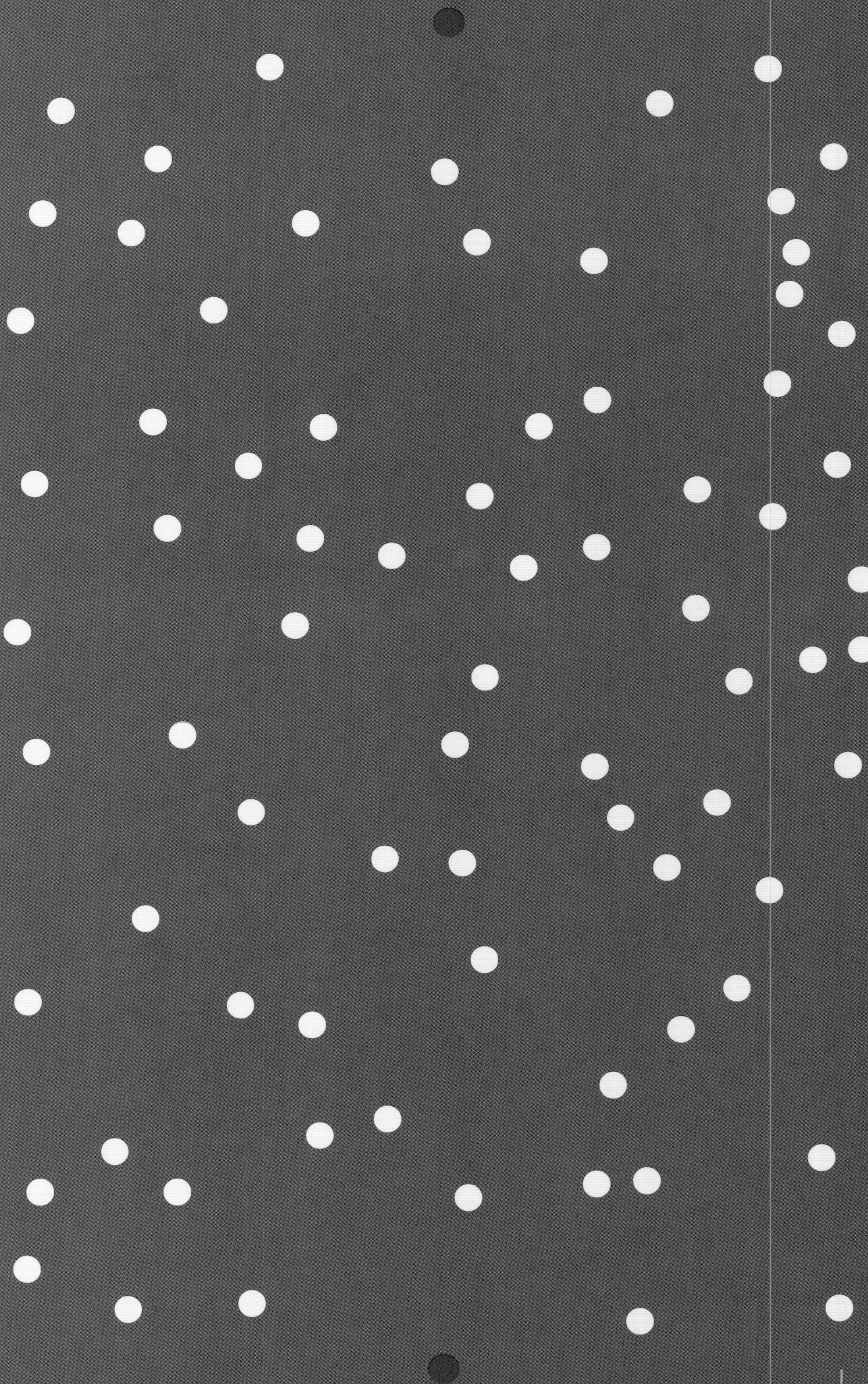

UTILITIES
HEXAGON

Join color to color using the color strips, forming six continuous lines. Lines formed by more than one stick are touching in one point without overlapping. The stick can overlap the colored areas.

Playing Pieces

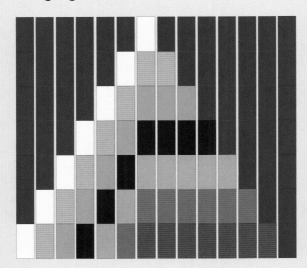

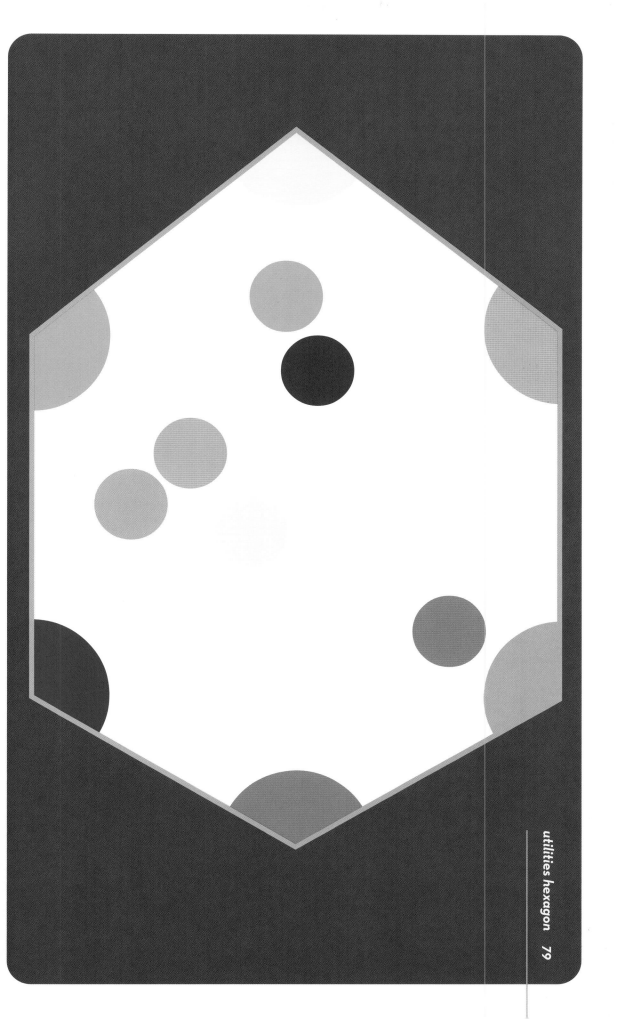

BIN PACKING GAME

One player plays with round tiles, the other with square tiles. The initial and end configurations of the playing pieces are shown below. Circles move from left to right, and squares from right to left. The top pieces move into the next column. Pieces may jump (and multiple jump) over pieces of a different shape. Multiple jumps count as one move.

A sample game is shown below with the player playing the square pieces winning in 58 moves.

PUZZLE

What is the smallest number of moves in which the positions of the circular and square pieces can be exchanged?

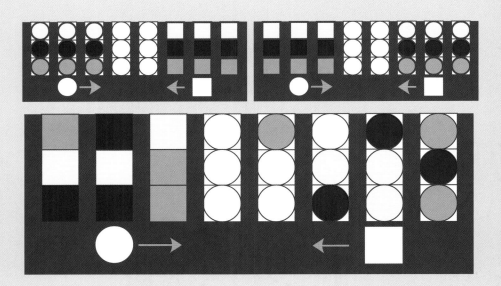

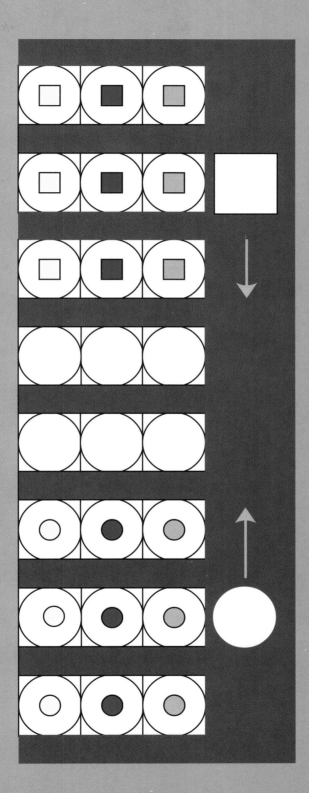

ICOSAHEDRON ROUTE

Can you visit every circle on the game board in succession without passing through any interconnecting line more than once?

This is equivalent to the problem of visiting each vertex of an icosahedron.

The game board is based on a two-dimensional plane diagram of the three-dimensional solid.

Notes:
1. It is not necessary to end the route adjacent to the point where you started.
2. It is not necessary to traverse all the lines of the game board (edges of the icosahedron).

If the requirement were instead to traverse every line, could the puzzle be solved without traversing any line more than once?

Playing Pieces

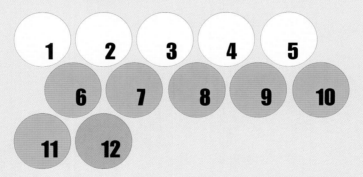

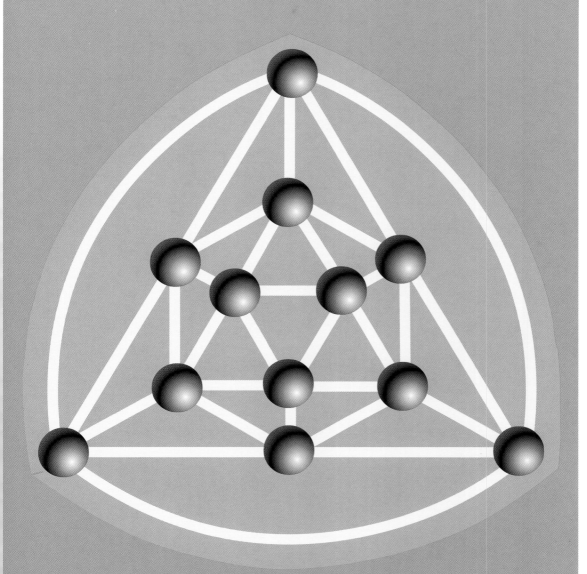

ANNIHILATION

Five fleets of starships are ready for combat: the yellow, orange, green, blue, and pink fleets, each consisting of six ships.

Your object is to distribute the 30 ships on the console screen, one ship in each square, so that when laser beams from all ships are fired horizontally, vertically, and diagonally, they hit only the enemy ships, and no beam hits a ship of one's own color. Laser beams will pass through empty squares, and stop once they hit a ship.

Playing Pieces

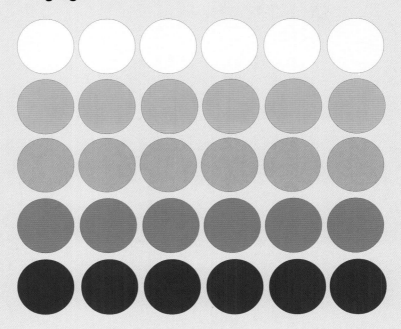

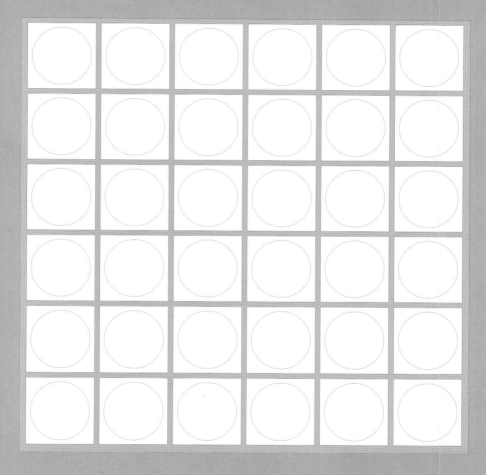

NIGHT CROSSING

A bridge will collapse in exactly 17 minutes. Four hikers must cross the bridge in pitch darkness. They have only one flashlight which is needed for each crossing.

At most, two people can cross the bridge at one time carrying the flashlight, which must be returned after each crossing.

Each hiker walks at a different speed; it takes the first hiker one minute to cross the bridge, the second two minutes, the third five minutes, and the fourth 10 minutes. Consequently, any pair of hikers crosses the bridge at the rate of the slower hiker's pace (so, for example, the first hiker crossing with the third hiker will cross the bridge in five minutes).

This is not a trick problem—the flashlight cannot be thrown back, no hiker is allowed to carry another, etc.

There are two possible solutions. Can you find both?

Playing Pieces

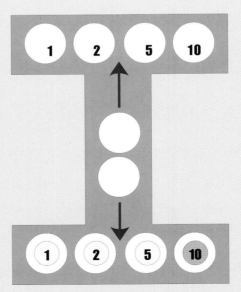

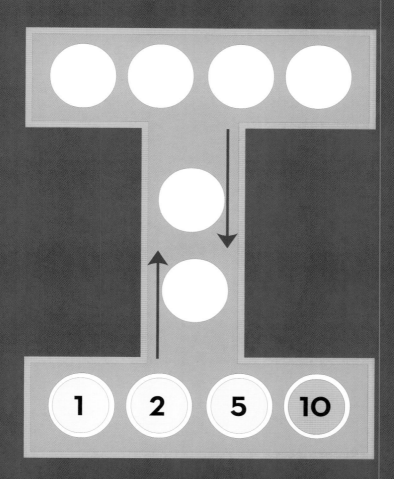

SOLITAIRE TRIANGLES

The traditional solitaire game has many variations; here is one of them.

Place a disc on every circle except the middle one.

Discs are being removed one at a time by jumping and removing the captured pieces.

Jumps can only be made along the lines.

The object is to end up with the last disc on the middle circle. Can you do it?

Playing Pieces

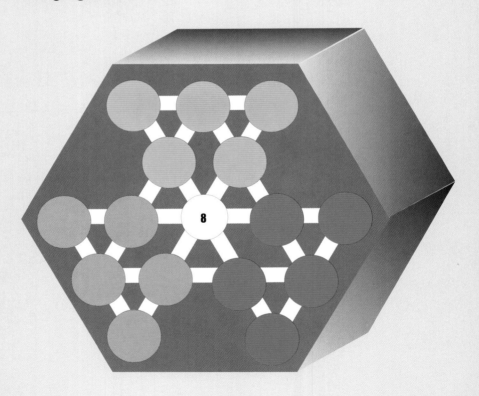

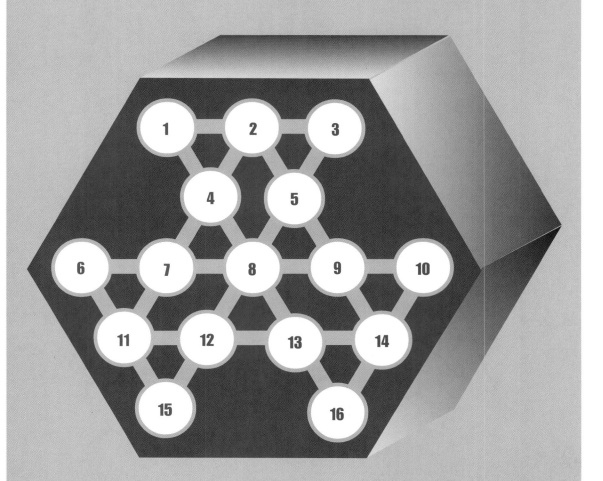

ELEVATION GAME

In this game, the board consists of six "floors," each accommodating up to five discs, and two transfer chutes (one for each player).

On the game board are 25 freely sliding discs in sets of five colors. The discs can be moved from the chutes on both sides into the floors and back again.

Game Objective:

The game is played by two players. Initially the five sets of discs are distributed randomly over the six floors by one player, in such a way that there are no two discs of identical color touching any floor. Floors may be filled, filled in part, or left empty. After the initial setup, the other player starts the game.

The object is to get sets of five identically colored discs on the same floor. A completed floor scores a point for the player creating it.

How to Play:

Players alternate moves. A move consists of two consecutive stages.

Stage 1 | Sliding, one by one, the three nearest discs from any floor or floors into a player's chute.

Stage 2 | Redistributing the three discs in succession back into any floor or floors.

There is one more rule to observe:

When two or more identical color discs are adjacent, they may not be separated, though they can be moved as one solid block. Moving the block counts as moving a single disc.

A game is ended when all the floors are completed or when no further moves are possible.

The subtlety and strategies of Elevation will be revealed after playing the game a few times. It was voted Game of the Year in France in 1980.

Playing Pieces

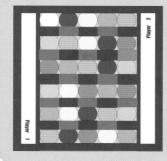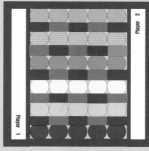

Elevation Game

Left: *One of the random initial configurations.*
Right: *A finished game with five floors completed.*

Player 2

Player 1

GANYMEDE CIRCLE

The circumference of the circle is divided into 31 equal segments. Can you place six markers along the circumference so that every distance from 1 to 31 will correspond to a distance between two marked points?

Playing Pieces

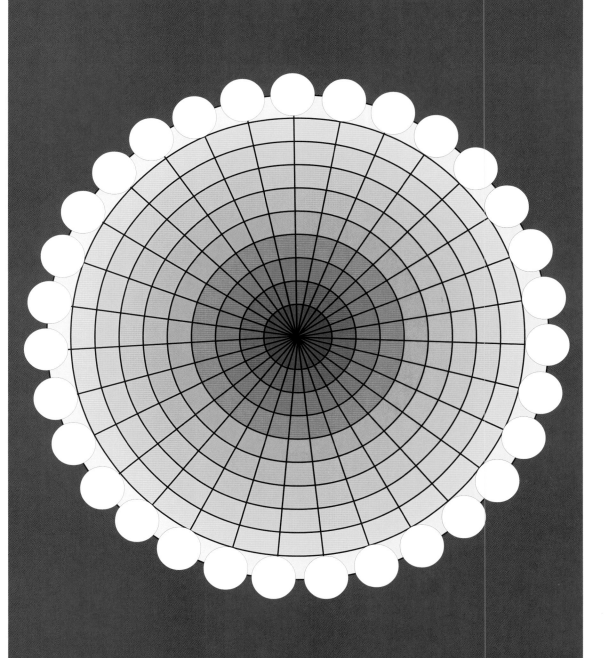

INCREASING-DECREASING

PUZZLE 1

Can you arrange the nine numbers, according to their numerical value, in the nine vertical columns of the game board as shown in the sample below (in an ascending sequence of nine numbers), but so to create ascending and decreasing sequences of three numbers, avoiding an ascending or decreasing sequence of four numbers?

Note: The sequences may or may not consist of adjacent numbers, as shown in the solution sample, but have a descending sequence of four numbers, which is wrong.

PUZZLE 2

Would a solution be possible for the above problem with ten numbers?

Playing Pieces

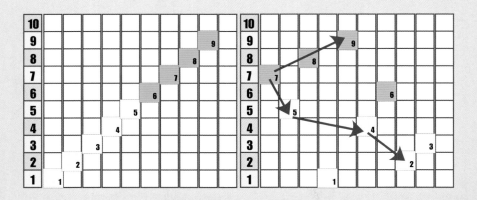

10										
9										
8										
7										
6										
5										
4										
3										
2										
1										

SEPARATING BUTTERFLIES

Using five straight lines, can you separate the 14 butterflies into 14 separate compartments, with each compartment containing one single butterfly?

In the example below, five lines were drawn, but only five butterflies were completely separated, while the rest are occupying compartments containing more than one butterfly each.

The sticks are allowed to overlap while creating the separating compartments.

Playing Pieces

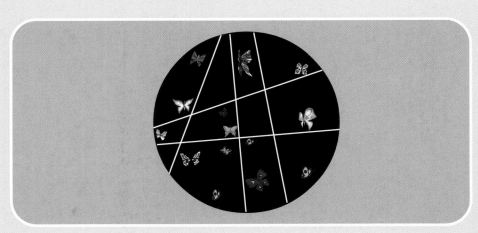

ROOK'S TOUR

A rook is initially placed as shown at right. The goal is to find a path of maximum length and covering as many fields as possible, changing course exactly 15 times. Dudeney was convinced that his solution below is the best, covering a length of 76 squares and visiting 61 squares. Is it? Can you do better?

Playing Pieces

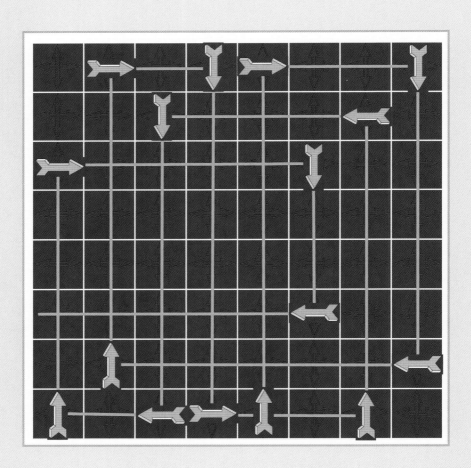

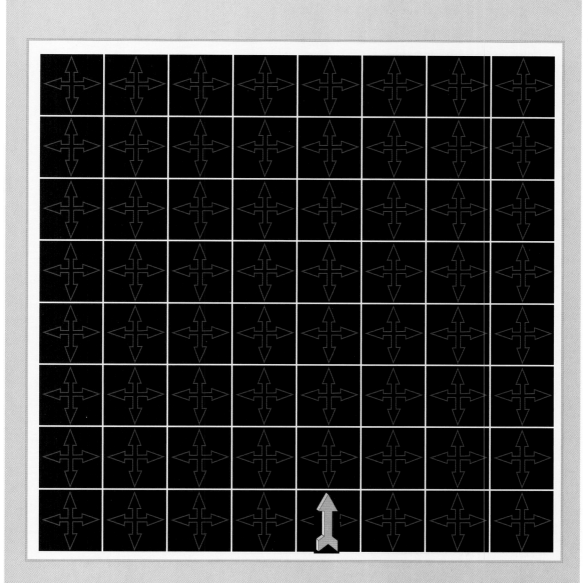

ELEVATOR TRIPS

In the 19-floor building there is only one strange elevator and it has only two buttons: "up" and "down." The "up" button takes you up eight floors (or doesn't move at all if it is impossible to go up eight floors), and the "down" button takes you down 11 floors (or doesn't move if it is impossible to go down 11 floors).

Is it possible to get from the lobby to any floor by taking the elevator?

How many times will you have to push the buttons to get from the lobby to all the other floors, and in what sequence will you visit all the floors?

Playing Piece—The Elevator

19																		
18																		
17																		
16																		
15																		
14																		
13																		
12																		
11																		
10																		
9																		
8																		
7																		
6																		
5																		
4																		
3																		
2																		
1																		
0																		

ROUNDABOUT

A Game For Two Players

Each player has three playing pieces of the same color, and the starting positions of which are marked on the game board.

Players take turns moving one piece at a time in any direction into the next empty space. A piece may jump over any other piece into an empty space beyond it, and making multiple jumps with one piece is also allowed. The jumped pieces are not removed.

The winner is the first player to get all three of his colors into the opponent's marked cells.

It should be noted that a player may not place any of his pieces in the opponent's marked cells until all three of his own colors have left their starting positions.

Playing Pieces

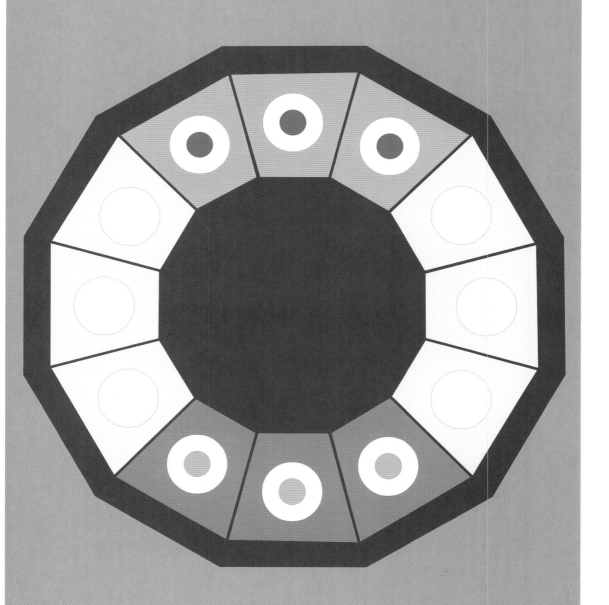

INSECT PATH

How many of the insect cells can you visit without going through any cell more than once?

You can start at any cell and move up, down, right, or left, but you may not move from one cell to a cell containing the same insect.

Playing Piece

PUSHOVER

A Two-Person Game

There are four sets of five playing pieces, two sets for each player. They are placed facedown, mixed, and then randomly distributed along the intersections of the game board facing up. Each player randomly chooses two color sets. Players alternate moves along a straight line. The object is to push the opponent's pieces off the board. More than one piece can be pushed overboard in one move. The winner is the player who pushes off all his opponent's pieces, or if no more captures can be made, the player with more pieces remaining on the board.

Playing Pieces

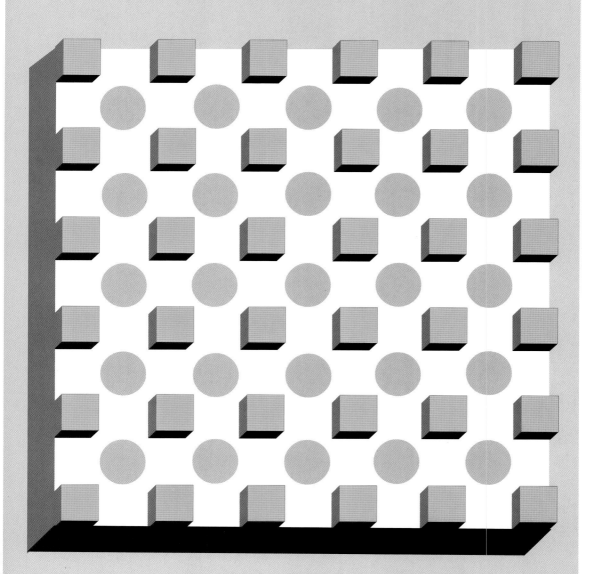

KNIGHTS' EXCHANGE

A Classic Chess-Knight Puzzle

The knights move as in chess. (That is, two squares in one direction, and one square in another direction. They can also jump over other pieces while moving.) What is the smallest number of moves it will take to exchange the places of the two sets of three knights?

Playing Pieces

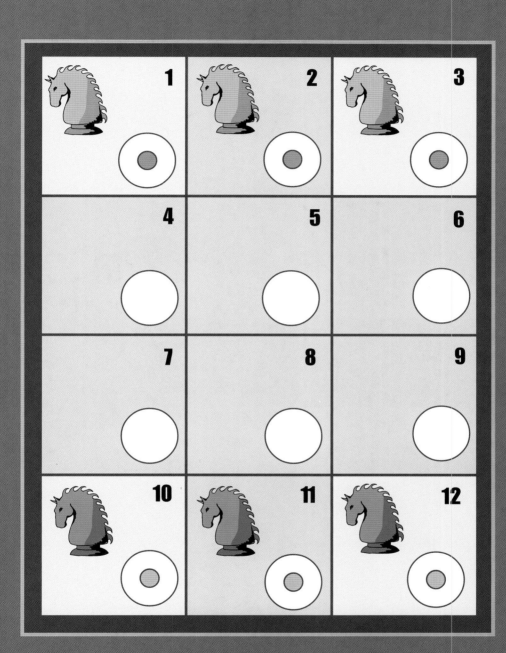

FIVE-IN-A-LINE

Each player has a set of 10 playing pieces in two colors of their choice. The object of the game is to "sandwich" your opponent's piece, which upon removal will create a straight line of five connected pieces of your color set in the middle area between the two bases.

Players take turns, moving one space horizontally or vertically into an empty space. Players can jump over one adjacent piece to an empty space beyond it; the piece jumped is then removed. Another way to capture opposing pieces is to "sandwich" one or more opposing pieces between two of your pieces; the "sandwiched" piece is then removed.

Once playing pieces are moved from their home base lines into the playing area, they are not allowed back for the rest of the game.

To win, you must have five of your pieces in a row with an opponent's piece "sandwiched" in the row.

Playing Pieces

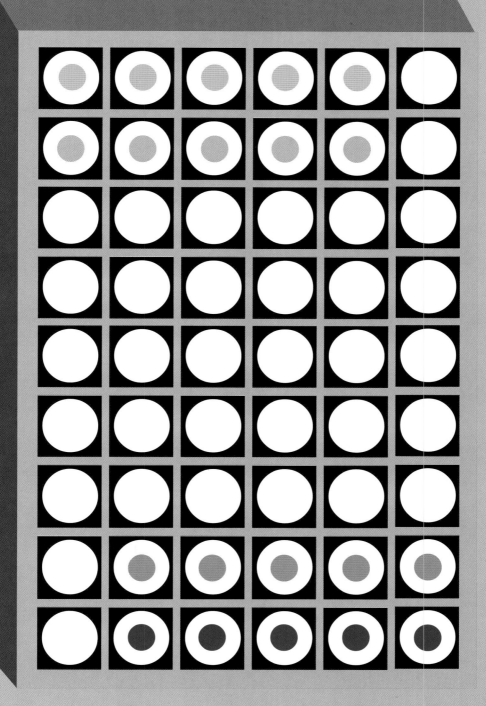

PEG SOLITAIRE

Peg solitaire is one of the most popular single-person games. Its origin is attributed to a prisoner of the Bastille, in France.

There are many variations of the game.

The object is to remove all pieces but one in a series of jumps, and end with the last piece in the center cell.

A "jump" consists of moving a counter over any horizontally or vertically adjacent counter, removing it, and landing on the next empty cell. Diagonal jumps are not allowed. Each move must be a jump, and a chain of continuous jumps counts as one single move. The color of the pieces does not matter.

PUZZLES 1 AND 2

Start with the patterns shown and end with the last counter in the center.

Puzzle 1

Puzzle 2

Playing Pieces

> "The game Solitaire pleases me much."
>
> —Gottfried von Leibniz, in 1716

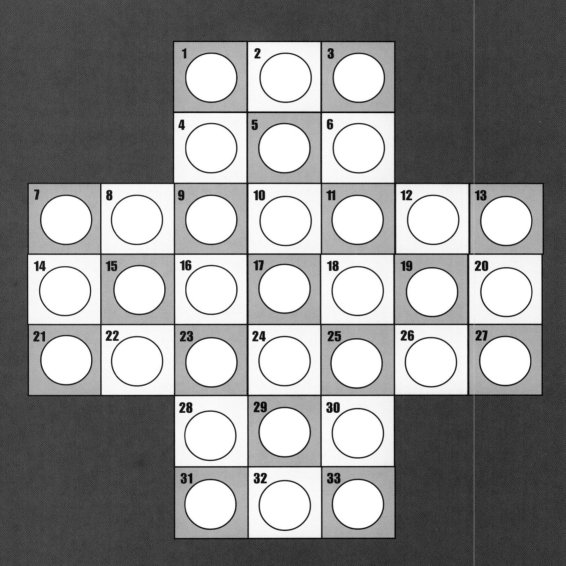

SOLITAIRE SQUARE

Solitaire problems have been devised on boards other than the standard solitaire game board. Noble D. Carlson, an engineer from Ohio, posed the problem:

What is the smallest square solitaire board on which it is possible to start with a full board except for a counter at one of the corners, and end up with a single counter?

Analyzing this problem, it was shown that solutions are possible on all square boards whose sides are multiples of three (except the 3-by-3 square). Therefore, the smallest solvable square board is the 6-by-6 (and solving it is not an easy task).

Carlson found a solution requiring 29 moves, but John Harris of Santa Barbara, California, a reader of Martin Gardner's column, came up with a 16-move solution.

In how many moves can you solve the 6-by-6 square board problem?

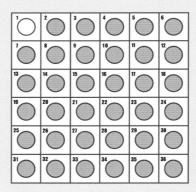

Playing Pieces

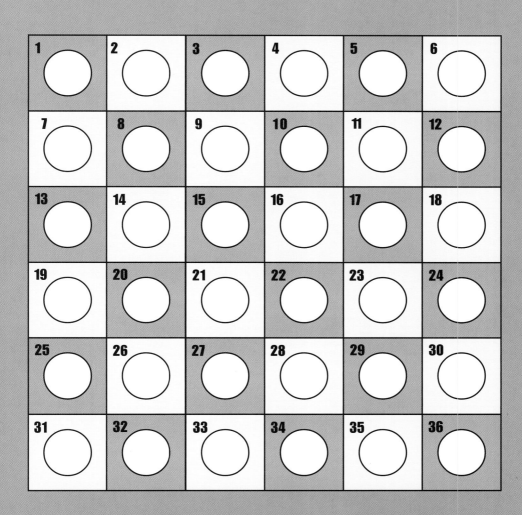

COLORING GRAPH

How many colors will you need to color each line segment between two grey end points so that no two lines of the same color meet at any end point?

Are three colors sufficient?

Playing Pieces

Edge-Coloring of Graphs

The problem of edge-coloring of graphs arises in a great variety of scheduling applications, typically associated with minimizing the number of noninterfering rounds needed to complete a given set of tasks.

For example, consider a situation where we need to schedule a given set of two-person interviews. We can construct a graph whose vertices represent people, with the edges representing the pairs of people who want to meet. An edge coloring of the graph defines the schedule. The colors represent the different time periods, with all meetings of the same color happening simultaneously.

The minimum number of colors needed to edge-color a graph is called its edge-chromatic number or chromatic index.

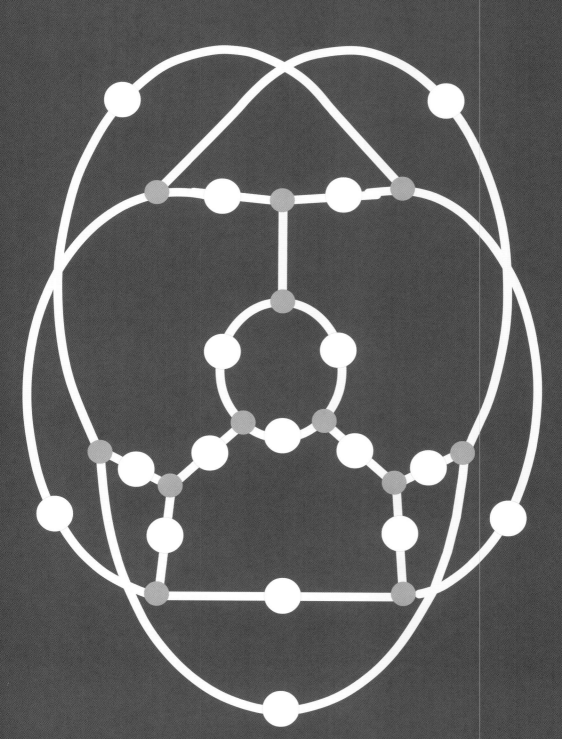

COLORING PATTERN

How many colors are needed for coloring each compartment of the pattern so that no two regions with a common border have the same color?

Can you do it with four colors?

Playing Pieces

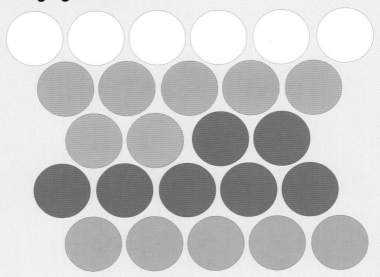

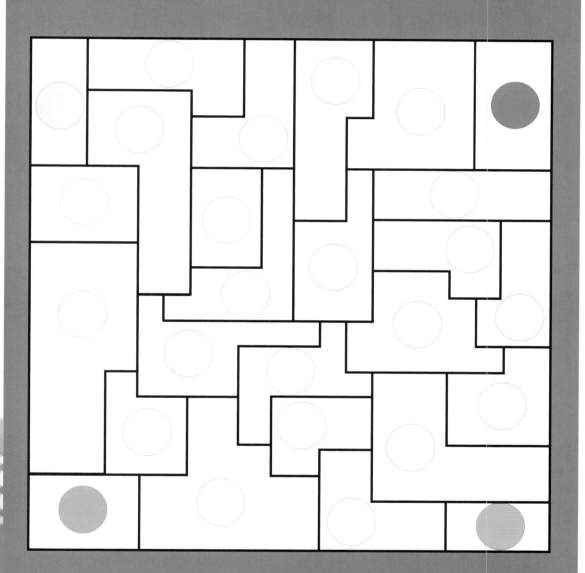

BEADS AND NECKLACES

Two-Color Necklaces of Seven Beads

Can you find and color the number of different two-color seven-bead necklaces?

Rotations and reflections should not be considered as different for this problem. The problem is equivalent to the number of different ways the sides of a heptagon can be colored.

 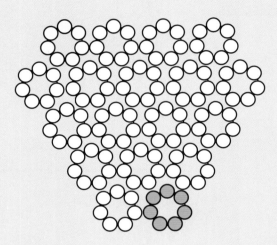

Playing Pieces

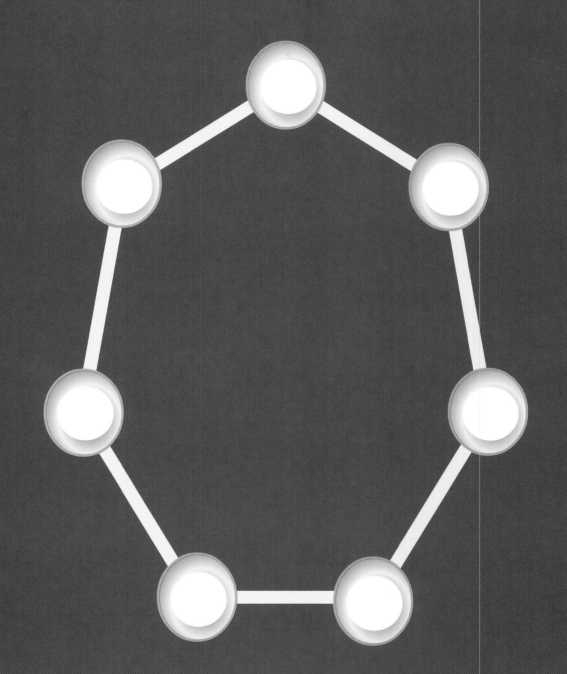

HYDE'S GAME

A checkers-variant for three players. Each player has six pieces as shown. Players advance their pieces one dark triangle at a time towards their opponents' corners, as shown by the arrows.

Capturing is the same as in conventional checkers. Multiple jumps are allowed. Background moves are not allowed except in multiple jumps.

After one player has been eliminated, the game continues until only one player remains.

Playing Pieces

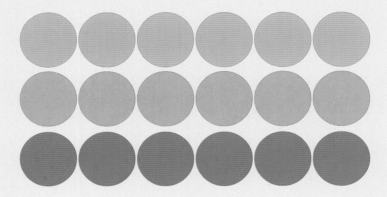

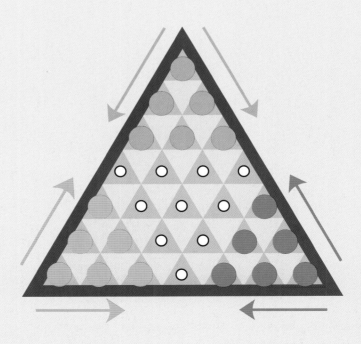

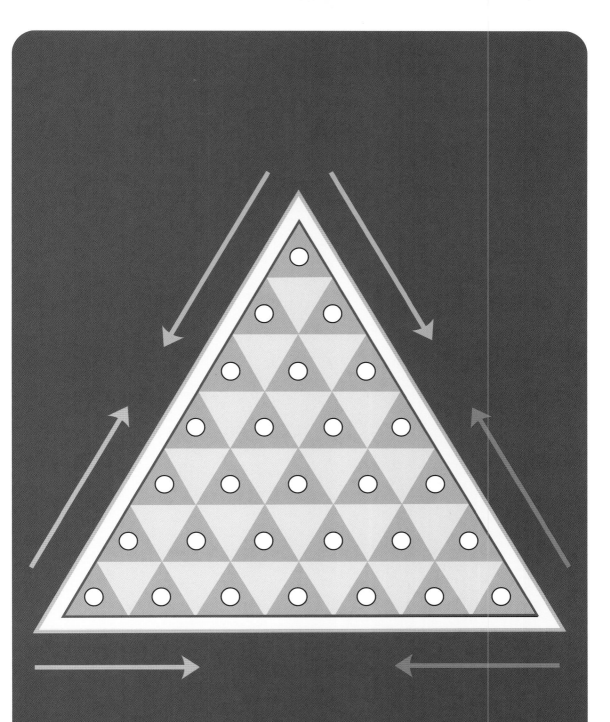

NUMBER CAROUSEL

Eleven consecutive numbers are distributed along the outer carousel as shown. Can you distribute the same discs in the inner carousel, so that no matter how you revolve it, or even invert it, there will always be only one pair of matching numbers on any radial line, while all the others will be different?

Playing Pieces

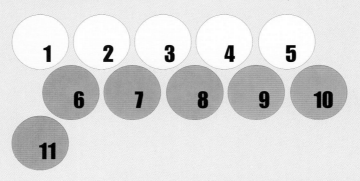

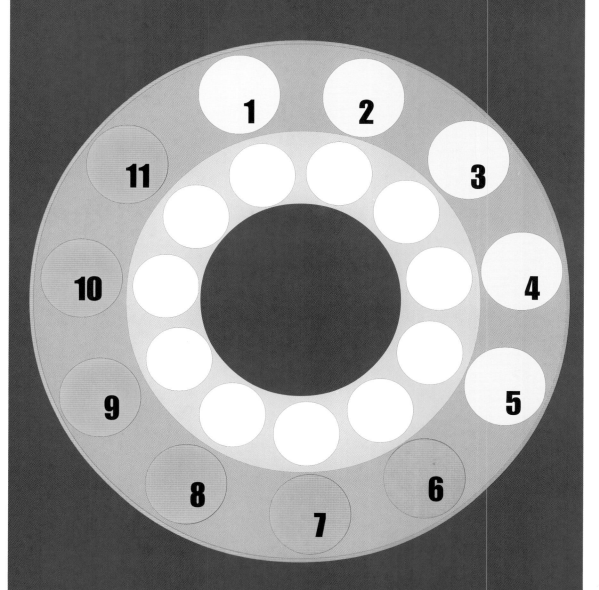

PACKING CIRCLES IN CIRCLES

PUZZLE 1

Can you place 11 circles in the smaller circle without overlapping the pieces and without entering the gray area?

PUZZLE 2

Can you place 13 circles in the bigger circle without overlapping the pieces and without entering the gray area?

Playing Pieces

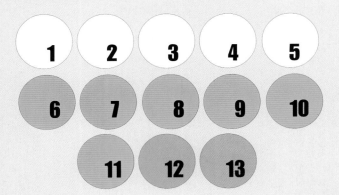

COLOR DOMINOES

The puzzle is to arrange the 28 color dominoes in the 7-by-8 game board to produce rows of four squares of the same color. There are 36 essentially different solutions, one shown below. Can you re-create the pattern with the 28 color dominoes?

How many other solutions can you find?

Playing Pieces

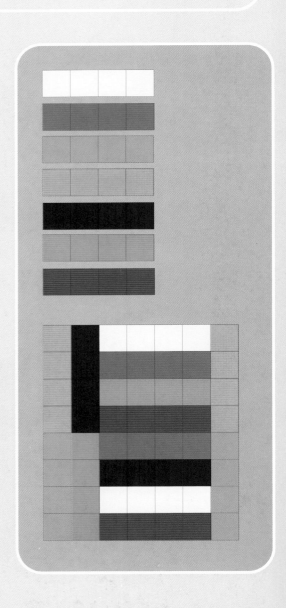

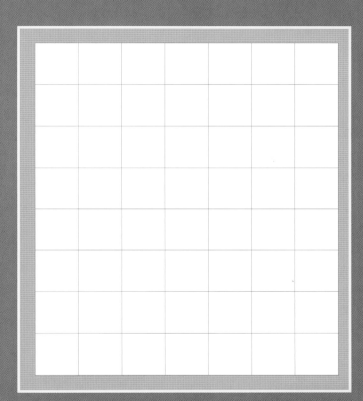

COLOR DOMINOES GAME

A Two-Person Game

The 28 color dominoes are mixed lying facedown. Players take turns placing a randomly chosen domino adjacent to a previously placed domino piece. Each horizontal row must consist of seven different colors.

The player who is forced to duplicate a color in a row is the loser. A completed game (tied) is demonstrated below.

Playing Pieces

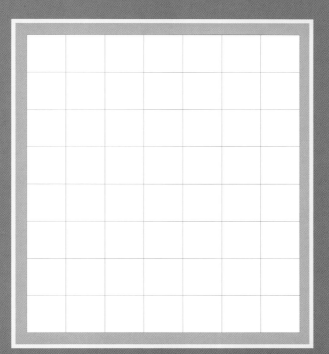

COLOR DOMINO MAGIC SQUARE & MAGIC RING

Color Domino Magic Square
Selecting a set of 18 color dominoes out of the set of 28, can you fill the 6-by-6 grid so that there are six different colors in each row and column?

Color Domino Magic Ring
Can you make a domino ring using the 28 color dominoes, matching the dominoes end-to-end in accordance with the rules of dominoes?

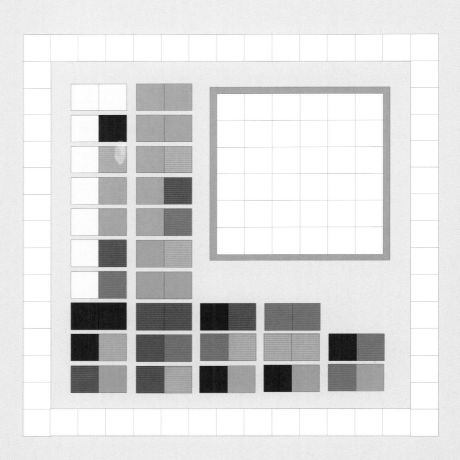

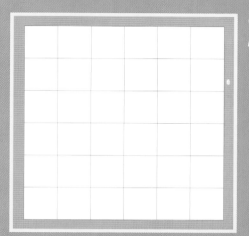

**Color Domino
Magic Square**

**Color Domino
Magic Ring**

COLOR MATADOR

The ultimate color domino puzzle

Solitaire Puzzle | Can you fit the 28 color dominoes into the 7-by-8 game board so that, apart from the yellow squares, there are 12 color blocks in any of the 2-by-2 square color configurations shown below.

Competition Game | Two players take turns, placing color dominoes adjacent to a domino piece placed earlier. Play the first domino wherever you choose. The first player unable to place a domino without disrupting the color scheme is the loser.

This was inspired by the Matador Puzzle, masterpiece of Fred Schuh (1875–1966), mathematician and great puzzlist.

Playing Pieces

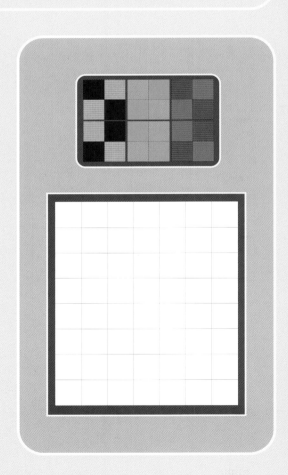

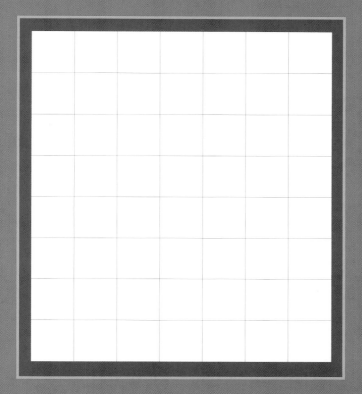

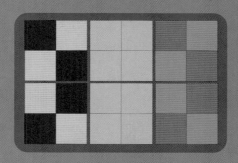

KNIGHTS OF THE ROUND TABLE

In how many different ways can eight knights be seated around the round table so that no one has the same pair of neighbors more than once?

One arrangement is shown with the knights numbered from 1 to 8. This is not an easy problem. There are 21 different arrangements. How many can you find?

Playing Pieces

1   2   3   4   5   6   7   8

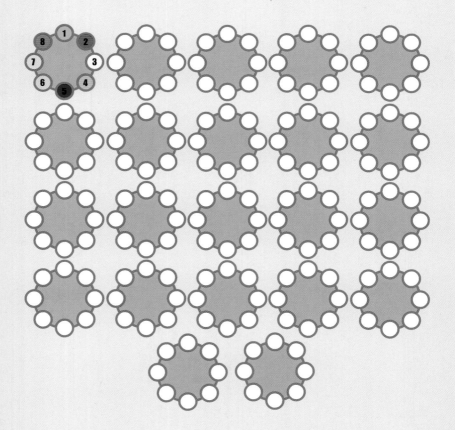

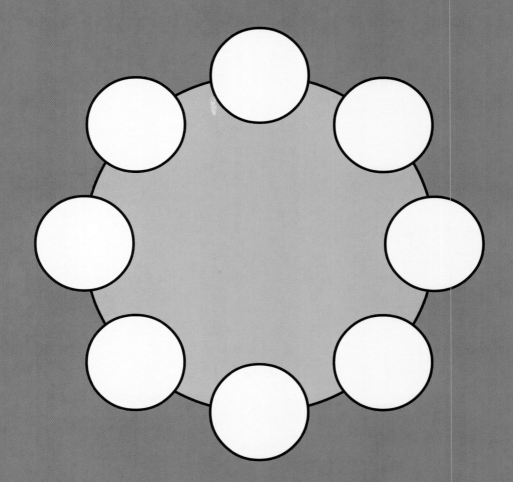

LINES OF ACTION

Lines of Action was invented in 1969 by Claude Soucie and received wide exposure in Sid Sackson's *A Gamut of Games*, published the same year.

The game is played on a standard checkerboard. Each player has 12 playing pieces which are initially set up as shown.

Pieces move in a straight line (vertically, horizontally, or diagonally) exactly as many spaces as there are playing pieces in that straight line.

Pieces cannot land on pieces of a player's own colors, but they can land on the opponent's colors, capturing them. Pieces may jump over pieces of one's own colors, but not over opposing pieces.

The object of the game is to arrange one's own pieces into a single connected group. Pieces are considered to be connected when they are in horizontally, vertically, or diagonally adjacent squares.

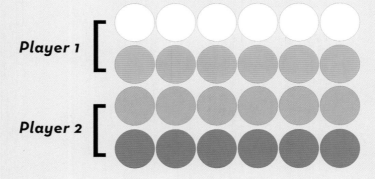

Player 1

Player 2

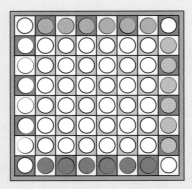

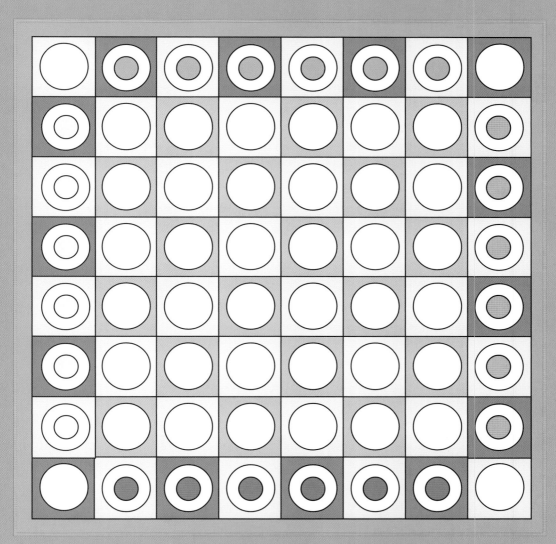

MAGIC
STRIPS

PUZZLE 1

Can you rearrange the 13 strips to form a configuration of seven rows of seven identical colors?

PUZZLE 2

Can you rearrange the 13 strips to form a configuration in which no color appears more than once in a horizontal row and vertical column?

PUZZLE 3

Can you again rearrange the 13 strips to form a configuration in which no color appears more than once not only in a horizontal row and vertical column, but also in all diagonals?

Playing Pieces

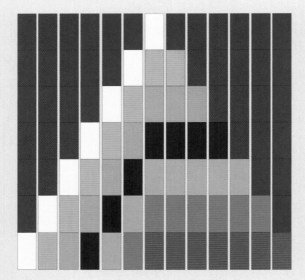

LAU KATI KATA

An Ancient Board Game from India for Two Players

Two sets of six playing pieces are set up as shown. Players take turns moving to any free adjacent circle. A piece may capture an adjacent enemy piece by jumping over it to an empty circle. Multiple jumps are allowed. Captures are obligatory.

The winner is the player who succeeds in capturing all the opponent's pieces.

Playing Pieces

 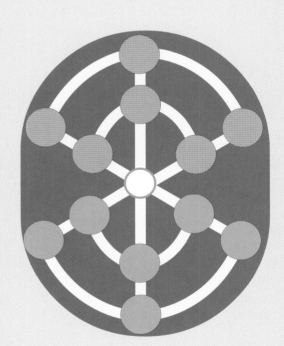

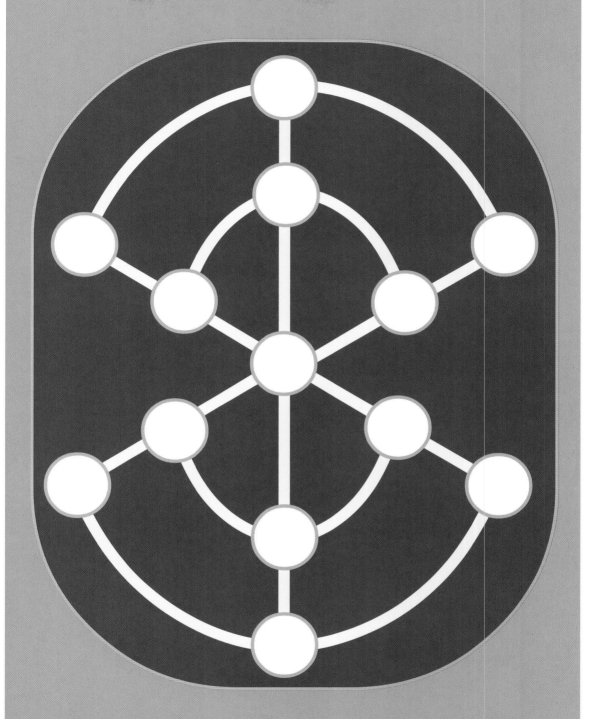

EGYPTIAN TRIANGLE

The surveyors of ancient Egypt, it is said, used the simplest right-angled triangle to construct near-perfect right angles. To obtain it, they divided a rope into 12 equal parts by knots. They used such a rope to form a triangle whose sides were in the ratio 3 : 4 : 5.

The triangle is often called the Egyptian Triangle, and is used to demonstrate the Pythagorean Theorem in its simplest form.

In such a triangle, one of the angles will be a right angle.

The Pythagorean Theorem states that $a^2 + b^2 = c^2$. Using the playing pieces, can you prove the validity of the Pythagorean Theorem for this specific triangle?

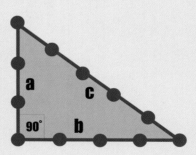

Playing Pieces

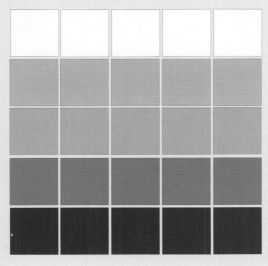

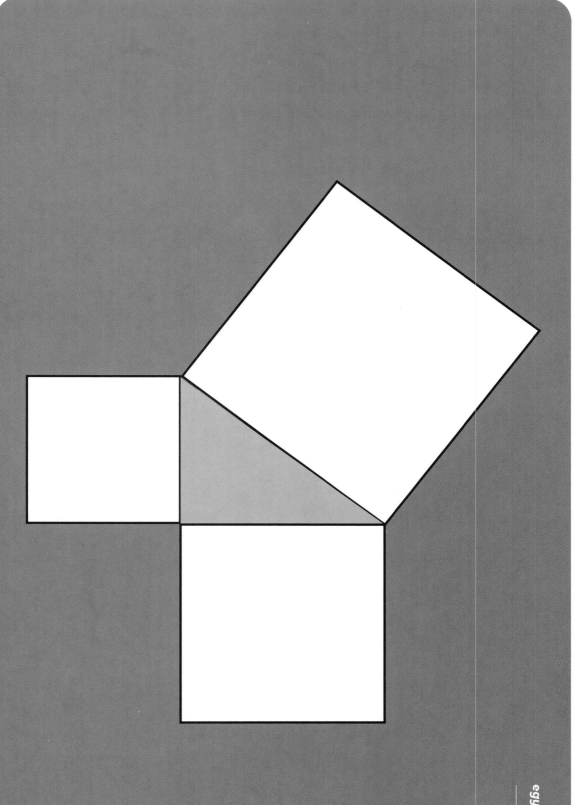

HEX WIN

This game is similar to Kensington. Each player has a set of 12 counters in two colors, yellow and orange for one player, green and blue for the other.

Players take turns placing their counters on the empty circles, trying to complete a triangle or square of their color.

When a player succeeds in creating a complete triangle or square which contains only pieces of his own colors, he is allowed to move one of his opponent's pieces.

When all the counters have been placed on the game board, a turn consists of sliding a counter along a straight line to an adjacent empty circle.

The first player to complete a hexagon in his own colors wins the game.

Playing Pieces

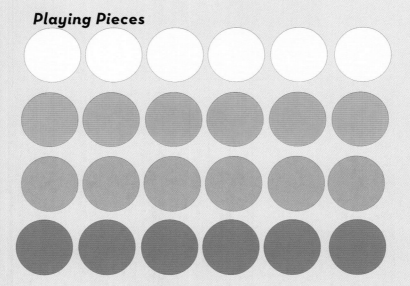

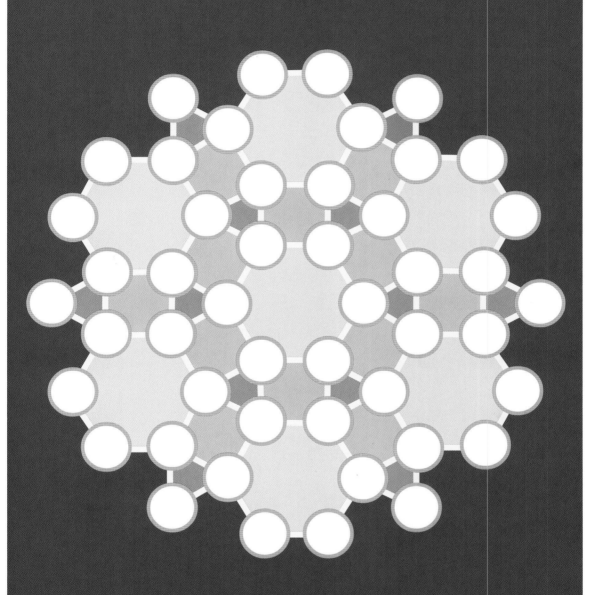

LONGEST PATH

The object of the puzzle is to travel from start to finish by moving the playing piece along the horizontal and vertical lines. On the first move, the piece moves one space; on the second move, it moves two; and so on, up to the fifth move. On the sixth move, the pattern repeats: 1, 2, 3, 4, 5 until reaching the finish line or until no more moves are possible. You can use a playing piece per move to help remember your path.

Two sample games are shown, one ending after four moves and another ending after five moves. What is the shortest solution you can find?

Playing Pieces

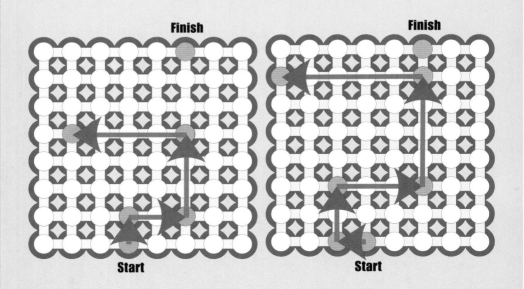

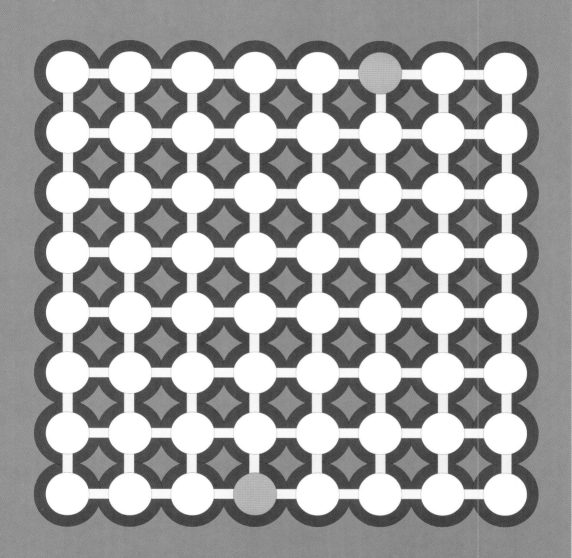

PACKING CIRCLES IN SQUARES

Eight Packing Puzzles

Pack the appropriate number of circles in the given outlines without overlapping, and without entering the green borders.

Playing Pieces

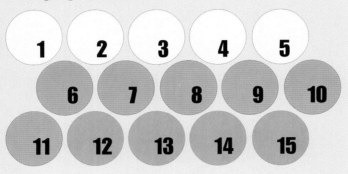

| 1 | 2 | 3 | 4 | 5 |

| 6 | 7 | 8 | 9 | 10 |

| 11 | 12 | 13 | 14 | 15 |

7	8	10
11	12	13
14	15

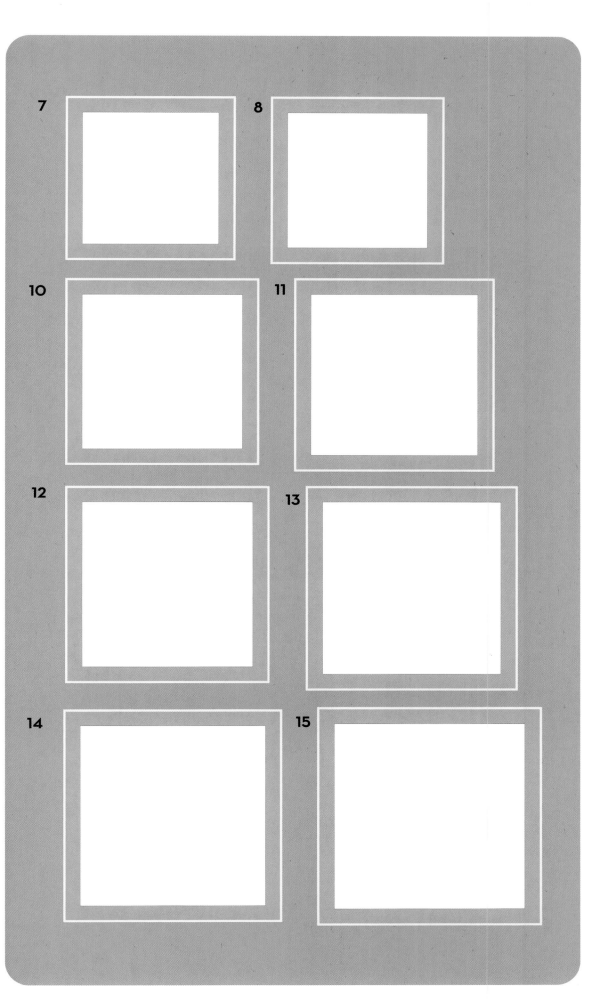

RAILWAY PUZZLE

Place nine counters in three colors as shown.

Moving only along the lines from circle to circle, arrange the pieces so there are three different colors on each circle and each straight line.

What is the minimum number of moves required to solve the puzzle?

Playing Pieces

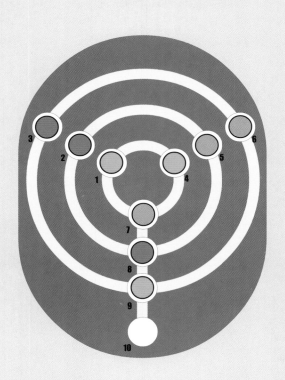

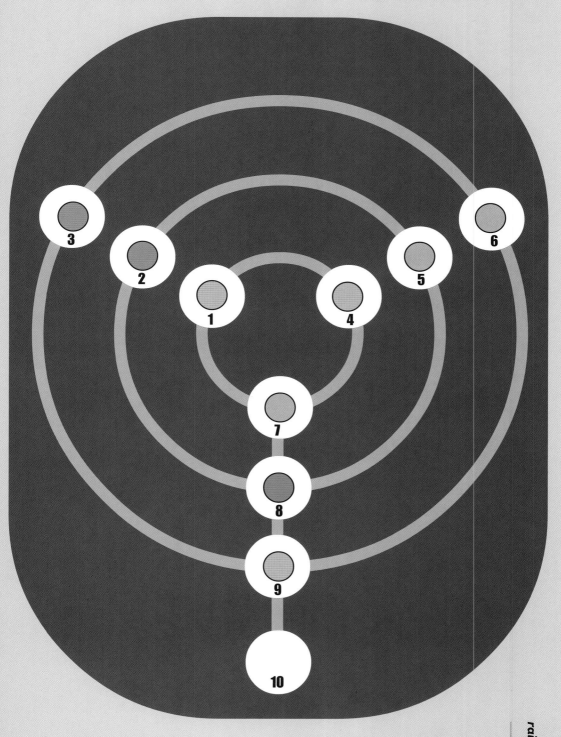

FARRELL'S SPIDER

Place the 18 discs on the web so that the sum of the numbers on each of the three hexagons and on each of the three ribs equals 57.

—Used with the kind permission of Jeremiah Farrell.

Playing Pieces

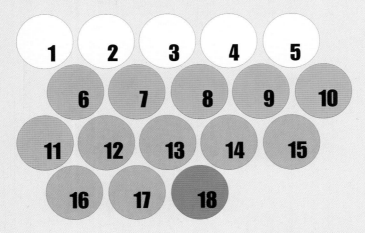

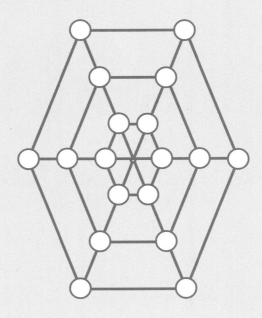

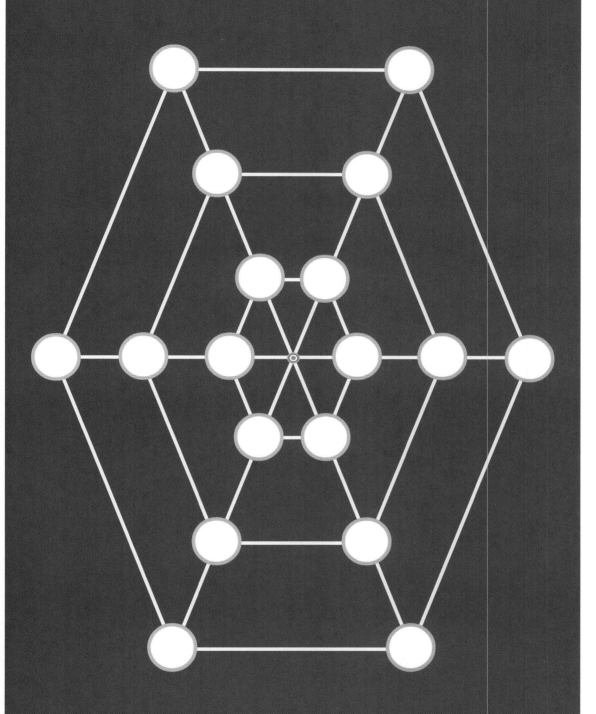

CELLULAR PATHS

In this puzzle, the goal is to make the longest path possible by moving according to the following pattern:

1. 1 square orthogonally
2. 1 squares diagonally
3. 2 squares orthogonally
4. Move along a 1 x 2 diagonal
5. 3 squares orthogonally
6. Move along a 1 x 3 diagonal
7. Continue in this fashion, until you reach the end.

The path may not cross itself, though it may land on or pass over the same square more than once. The maximum number of possible moves for 2 x 2, 3 x 3, 4 x 4, and 5 x 5 squares are shown. How many can you make on the 8 x 8 board at right (starting on the green square and ending on the red, as in the examples)?

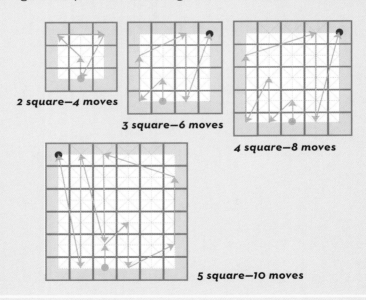

2 square—4 moves

3 square—6 moves

4 square—8 moves

5 square—10 moves

Playing Pieces

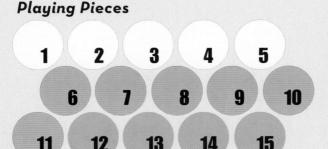

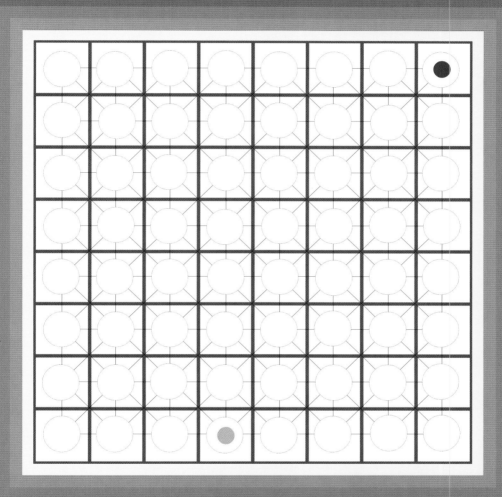

MAN OF LAW'S PUZZLE

Place the numbered counters on the squares as shown. Moving only along the lines from square to square, arrange the pieces in their correct numerical sequence, from 1 to 8, with a blank space at the bottom.

What is the minimum number of moves required to achieve a solution?

Playing Pieces

1
2
3
4
5
6
7
8

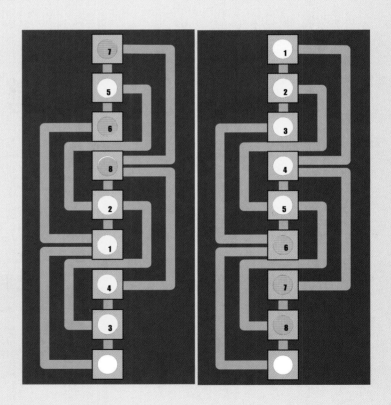

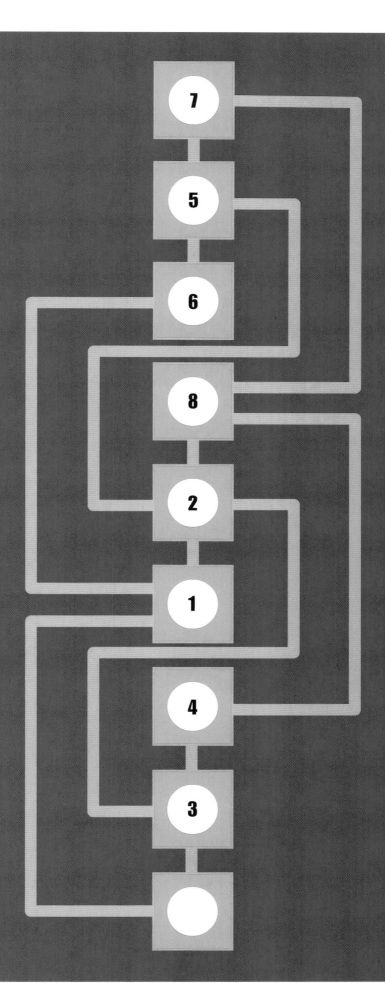

NUMBER LABYRINTH

A number labyrinth for a square grid of side n is a continuous sequence of numbers from 1 to n^2, traveling in ascending order through adjacent squares, with one number in each square.

In the grids shown here, some cells are occupied. The 4 x 4 grid has been filled in as an example. Can you complete the 5 x 5 grid?

4 X 4

	7		
	1		

6	7	8	9
5	4	3	10
16	1	2	11
15	14	13	12

5 x 5

5				
			23	20
	9			14

Playing Pieces

1	2	3	4	5
6	7	8	9	10
11	12	13	14	15
16	17	18	19	20
21	22	23	24	25

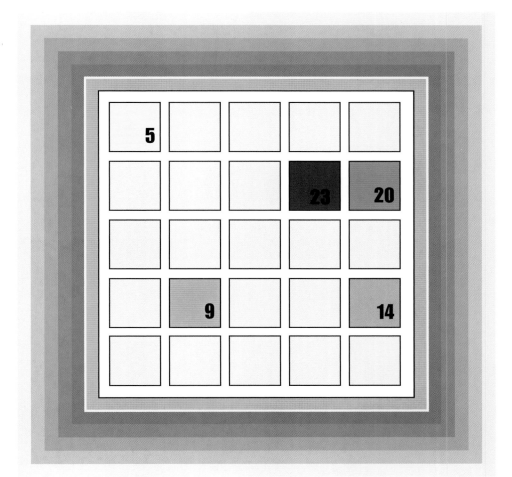

COUNTER PUZZLE

Exchange the positions of the orange and green counters, moving along the straight lines and stopping only on circles. At no time may counters of different colors be on the same straight line.

Counters may move as far as they like on a straight line, and may cross a line on which a different color rests, but cannot stop there.

Playing Pieces

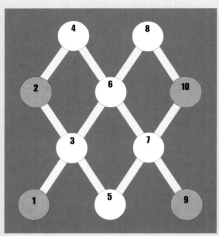
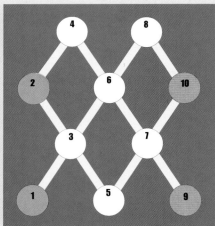

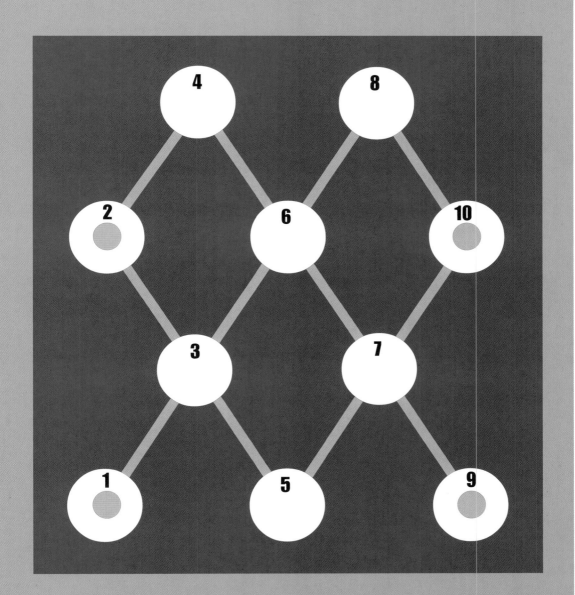

NUMBER NEIGHBORS

Can you place the numbers from 1 to 9 on the circles of the game board so that the sums of the numbers that are their connected neighbors are as the arrows indicate?

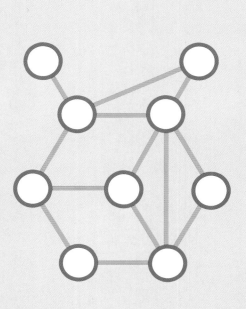

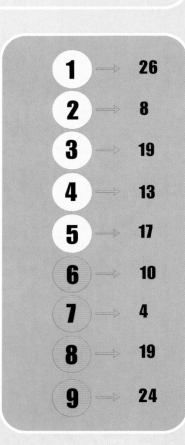

1 →	26
2 →	8
3 →	19
4 →	13
5 →	17
6 →	10
7 →	4
8 →	19
9 →	24

Playing Pieces

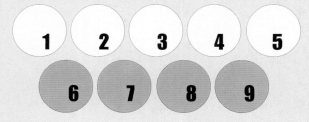

1 2 3 4 5
6 7 8 9

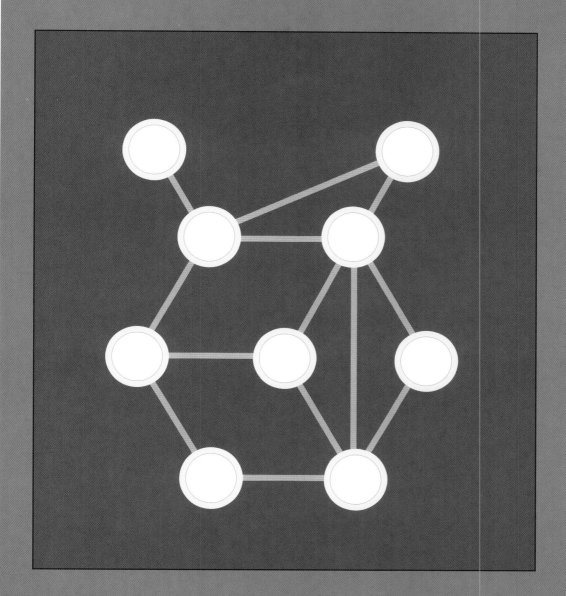

FOXES AND GEESE

Exchange the positions of the orange and green counters, moving only along the straight lines and stopping only on the circles. At no time may a fox and a goose be at the ends of the same straight line.

Playing Pieces

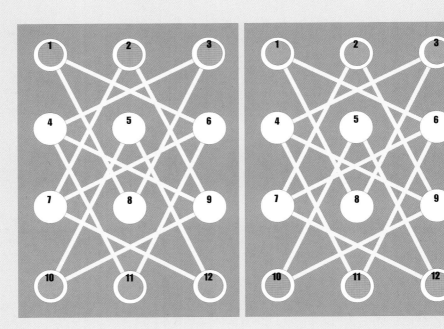

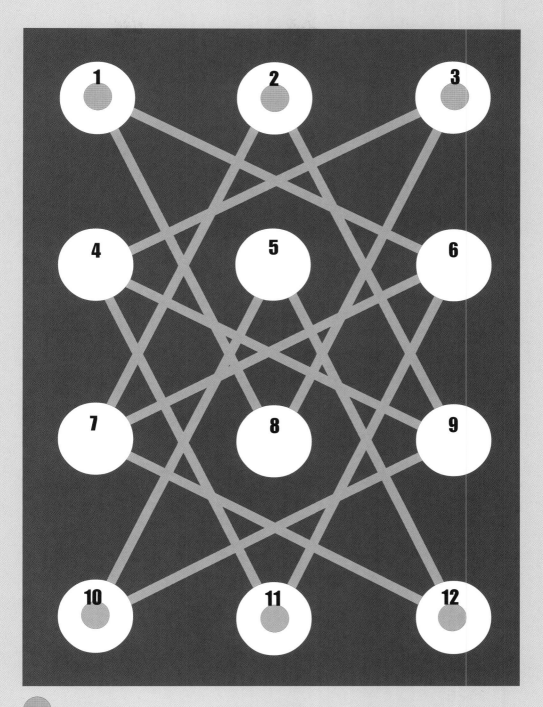

Foxes

Geese

NUMBER SUMS AND DIFFERENCES

Can you rearrange the ten numbers in a row so that each number (except those on the ends) is the sum or difference of its two neighbors?

Playing Pieces

"When you cannot express it in numbers, your knowledge is of a meager and unsatisfactory kind."

—Lord Kelvin (William Thomson 1824-1907)

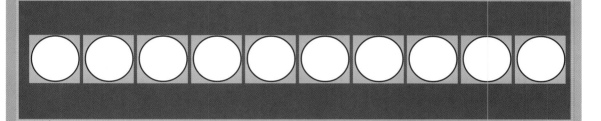

NUMBER BOXES

Can you distribute the two sets of numbers, from 1 to 21, in the seven column boxes, six numbers in each column, so that every number appears in two boxes, and every pair of boxes has exactly one number in common?

Playing Pieces

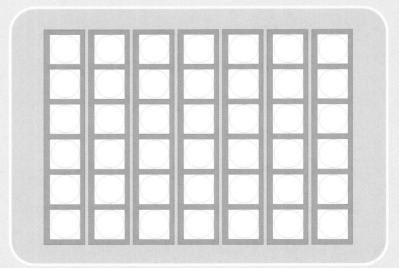

1	2	3	4	5
6	7	8	9	10
11	12	13	14	15
16	17	18	19	20
21				

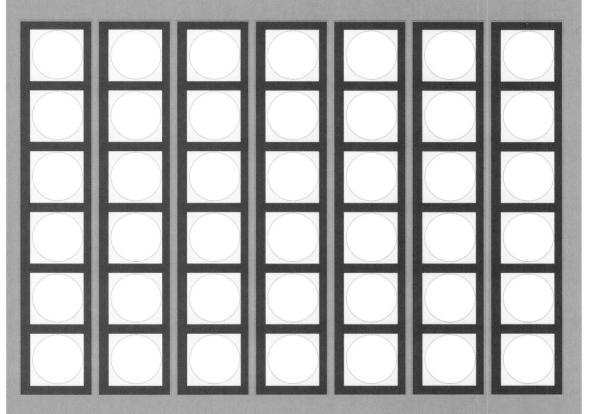

FOUR FROGS SWITCH

Exchange the positions of the two orange and two green counters in seven moves, moving only along straight lines and stopping only on circles. A counter may move any number of circles per move, provided none of the circles are occupied by another counter.

Playing Pieces

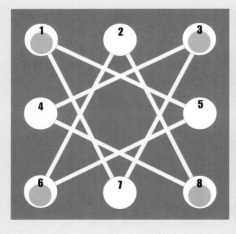
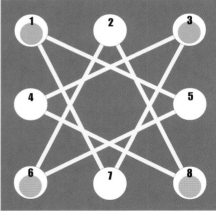

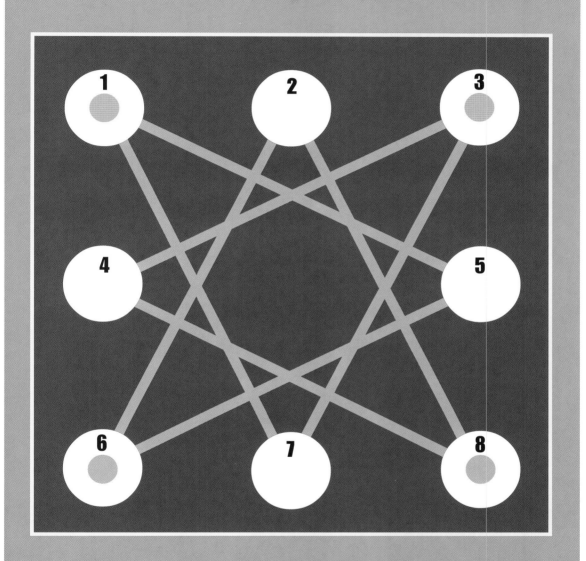

WEIGHTS IN THREE BOXES

What is the smallest number of boxes into which you can place consecutive weights, starting from weight 1 and up to weight n, according to the following rule: ***In no box should there be three weights of which one of the weights is the sum of the other two.***

How many weights can you place in three boxes following this rule?

Can you place 17 consecutive weights? If not, how many can you fit? Can you fit more than 17?

Playing Pieces

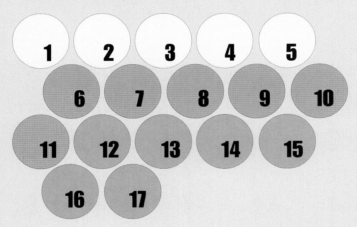

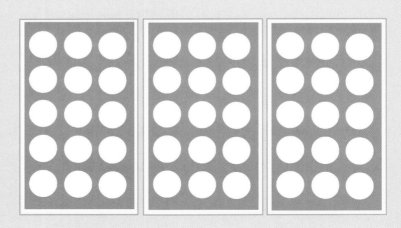

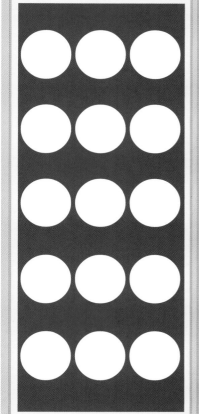
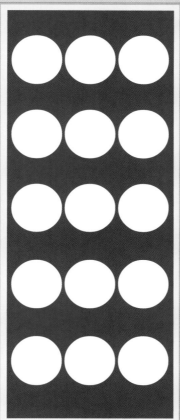
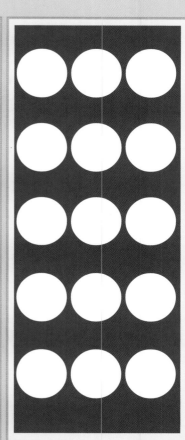

TRANSFORMATION SWITCH

Start with the number 1 at the top, and the 12 at the bottom. Arrange the numbers in order along the slanted slot with 1 at the left and 12 at the right. Discs may move any distance during a move.

What is the minimum number of moves required to achieve the switch?

Playing Pieces

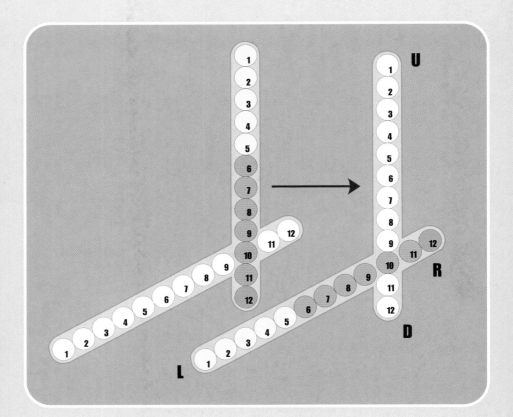

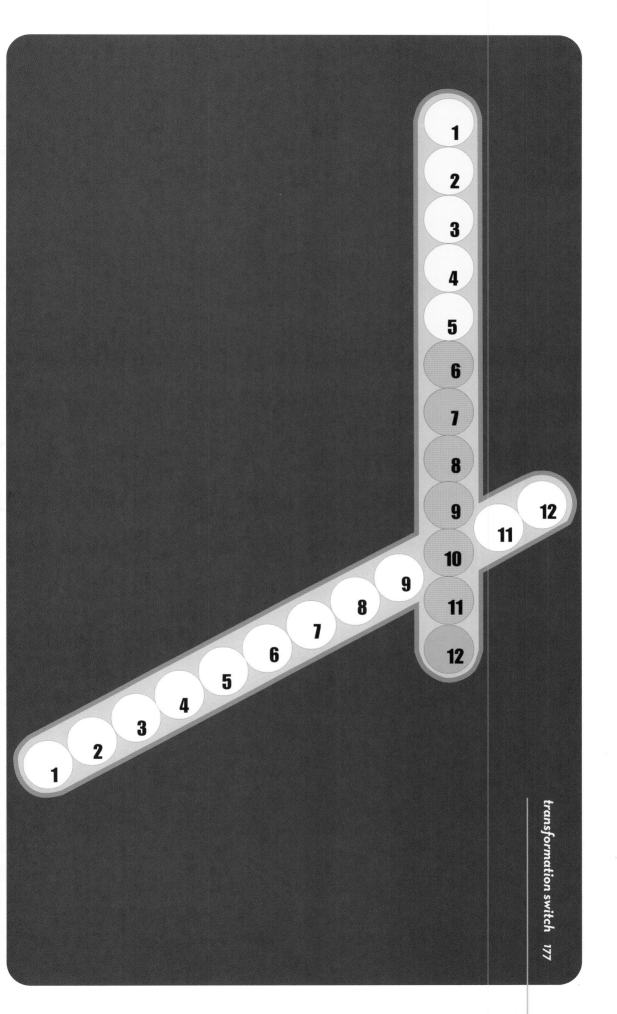

EXCHANGE MOVES

Two red counters and two green counters are placed on the game board, the red counters on the green circles and the green counters on the red circles as shown.

Move the counters alternately—first a red counter, then a green counter, and so on—along the yellow connecting lines from circle to adjacent circle so that they end up in the reverse positions, the red counters on the red circles and the green counters on the green circles.

What is the smallest number of moves required to achieve the switch?

Playing Pieces

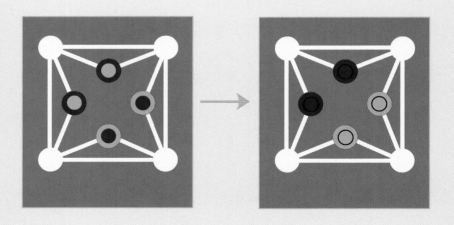

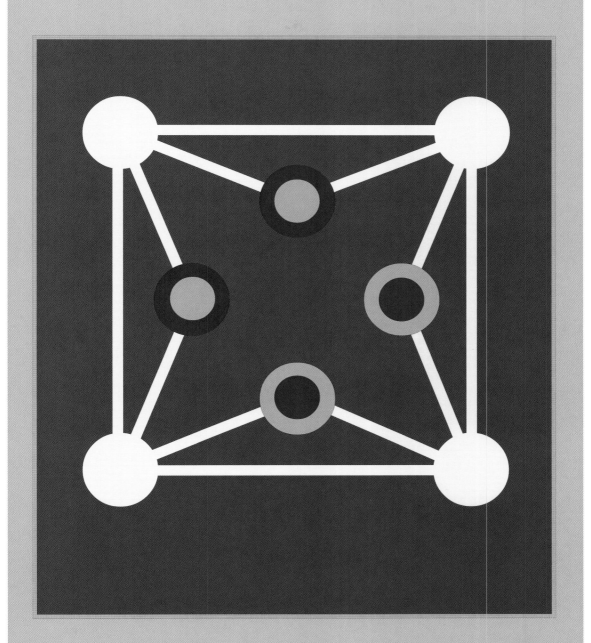

FROM CUBE TO CUBE

Start anywhere and find a path that steps on all blocks without stepping on any block more than once. You can move up or down one level at a time along two levels sharing an edge, or to an adjacent square on the same level.

Playing Pieces

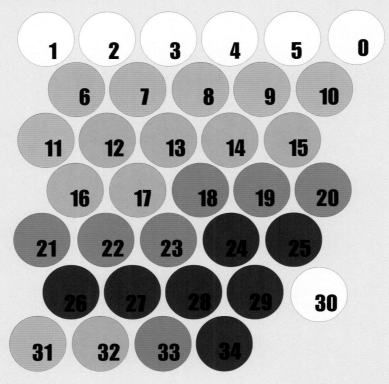

BLOCKING ROADS

First, see if you can visit the 14 circles in a continuous line along the white connecting lines, starting at any circle, visiting each circle just once, and returning to the point where you started.

Then, one by one, in succession, close one of the seven connecting roads with a diverting arrow (as shown in the example below, in which road 1 is closed).

Playing Pieces

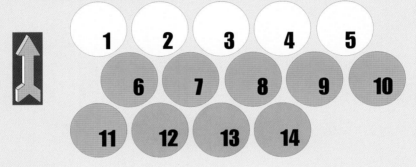

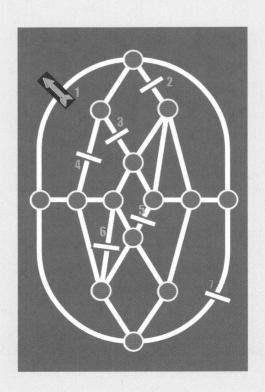

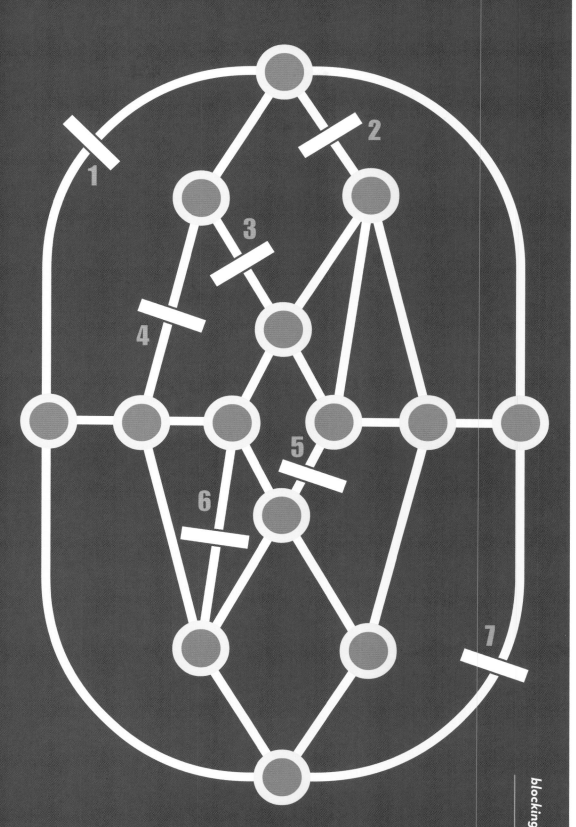

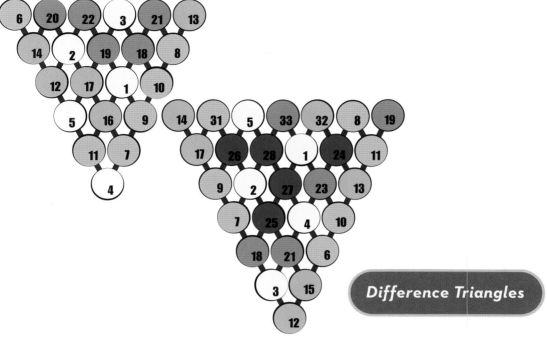

Difference Triangles

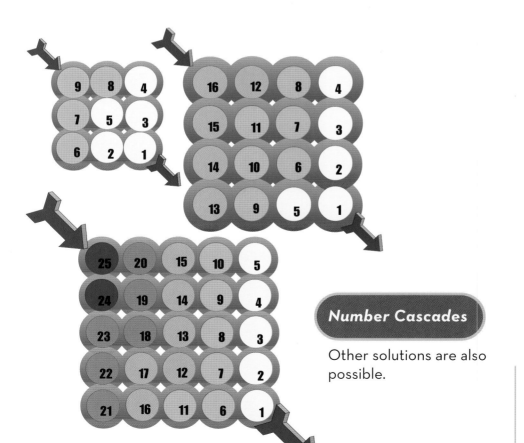

Number Cascades

Other solutions are also possible.

No-Two-in-a-Line Hexagon

Queen's Increasing Tour Problem

The maximum solution takes 14 moves and has a total length of $28 + 28\sqrt{2} = 67.59$ units, shown below.

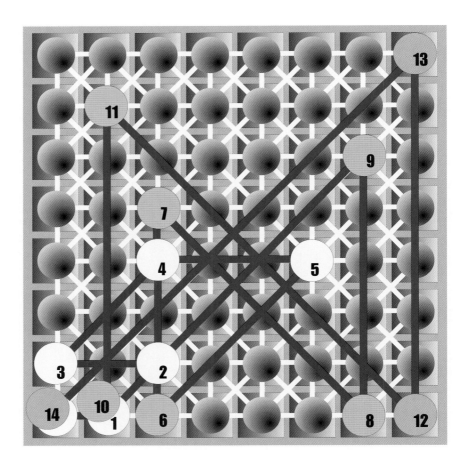

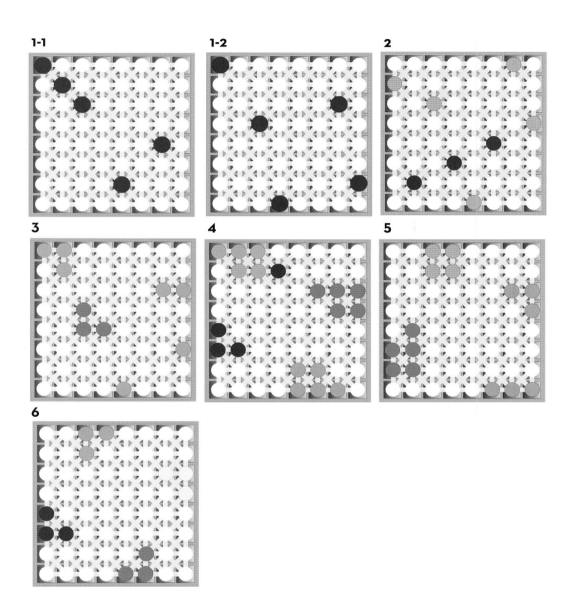

1-1

1-2

2

3

4

5

6

Puzzle 1—18 squares (solution found by Pertti Hamalainen in 1979)

Puzzle 2—26 squares

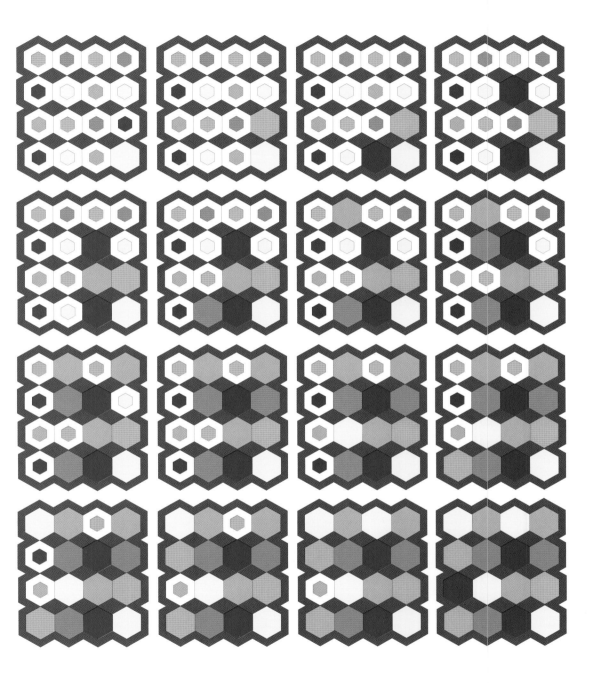

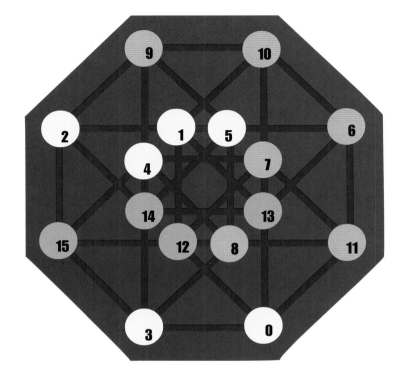

Graeco-Latin Magic Color Square of Order 4

One of the different possible Graeco-Latin squares of order 4.

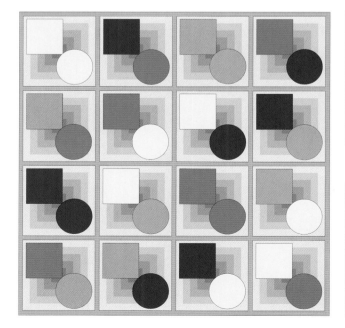

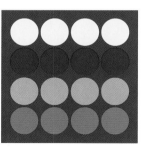

Graeco-Latin Magic Color Square of Order 5

One of the different possible Graeco-Latin squares of order 5.

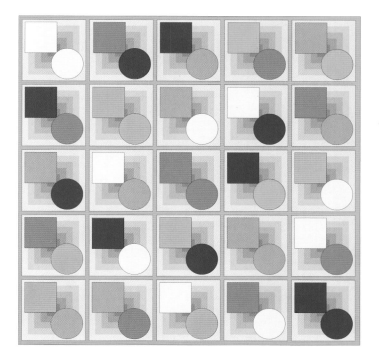

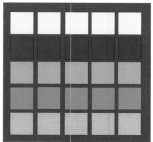

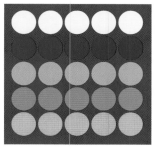

Arrow Number Puzzle 1

0	2	2	1	2	0
0	↗	↘	↗	↑	0
1	←	↗	↑	↓	1
0	↑	↘	←	↘	0
0	→	↑	↗	→	2
1	0	1	0	1	2

Arrow Number Puzzle 2

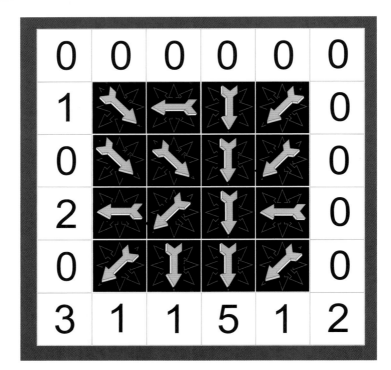

Arrow Number Puzzle 3

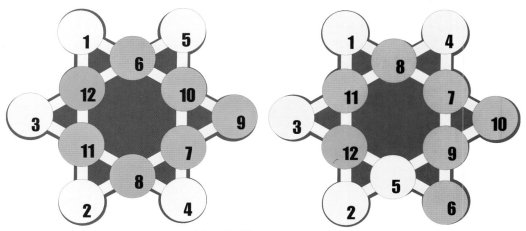

Magic Hexagram 1

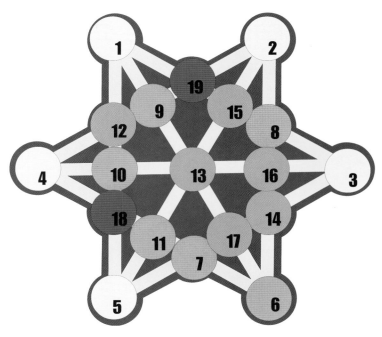

Magic Hexagram 2

One of the ten solutions in 30 moves:
1–2–5–8–7–4–8–5–2–8–3–1–8–2–5–7–4–3–1–6–3–1–
2–5–7–4–1–2–5–8

Bishops' Exchange

Twelve moves are necessary as shown.

1 ◯	2 ◯	3 ◯	4 ◯
5 ◯	6 ◯	7 ◯	8 ◯
9 ◯	10 ◯	11 ◯	12 ◯
13 ◯	14 ◯	15 ◯	16 ◯
17 ◯	18 ◯	19 ◯	20 ◯

	Orange	Yellow
1	18—15	3—6
2	17—8	4—13
3	15—5	6—16
4	8—3	13—18
5	5—10	16—11
6	10—4	11—17
7	20—10	1—11
8	10—13	11—8
9	19—16	2—5
10	16—1	5—20
11	13—7	8—14
12	7—2	14—19

Arrow Tours 1

In the solution below, only six squares were not visited.

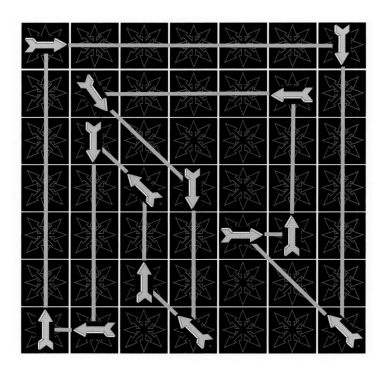

In the solution below all squares have been visited as shown.

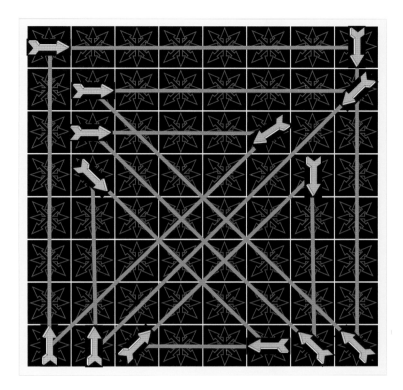

One of the possible solutions.

Q-Bits

Fifty basically distinct solutions of the Q-Bits color-matching solitaire puzzle. Rotations, reflections, and color reversals are not considered different.

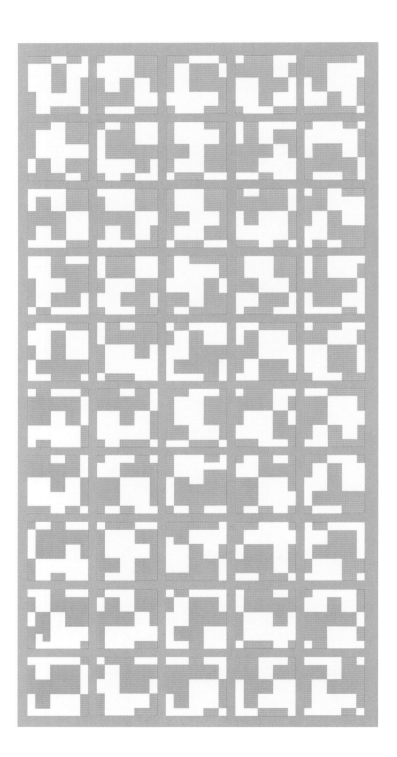

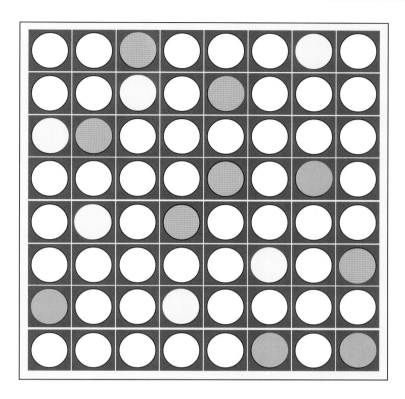

Puzzle 1

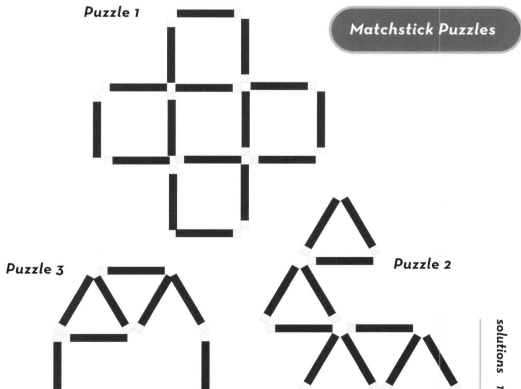

Puzzle 3

Puzzle 2

Tricky Discs

The minimum number of moves for two sets of five discs is 35. For two sets of 10 discs it is 120 moves.

The number sequence written beneath the playing pieces on the game board provides a general algorithm for any number of sets. It tells the number of successive alternating moves which must be made by each color group. If you follow this sequence, you will ultimately come to the solution in the fewest possible number of moves.

The sequence starts with one move by either of the center discs into the middle space. It is then followed by two moves by the discs of the other color, then three moves from the first set, etc.

Mathematically, the minimum number of moves can be seen as: **the number of discs in each set x (the same number + 2).**

For example, here is the number sequence for two sets of 10 discs: 1—2—3—4—5—6—7—8—9—10—10—10—9—8—7—6—5—4—3—2—1. The sum of this sequence is 120 (10 x 12 = 120).

Sneaky Slides

To place all eight pieces, remember that each time you place a disc on a circle, its end position should be the starting position of the previous piece. Using this strategy, there will always be one pathway free.

A practical approach involves first filling the graph with eight discs and playing the puzzle in reverse, noting the moves.

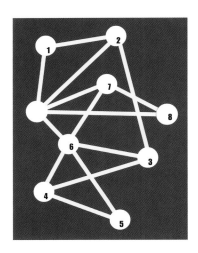 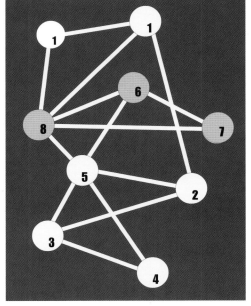

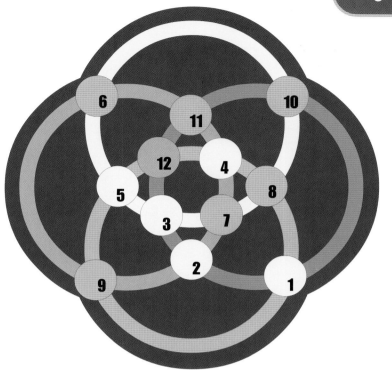

There are two distinct solutions.

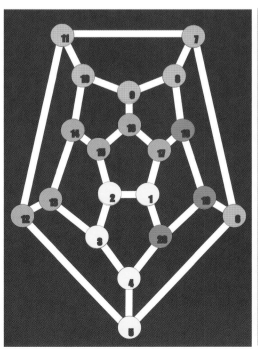 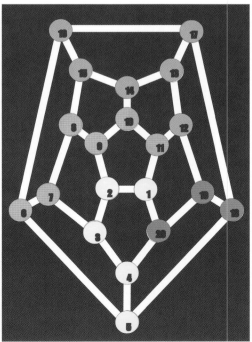

There are four solutions. One is shown below.

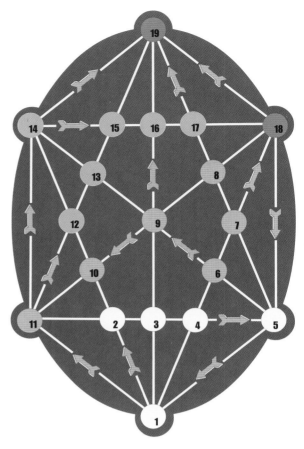

There are 86 solutions. One is shown below.

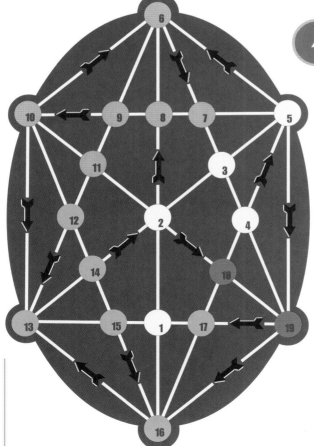

There are 86 solutions. One is shown below.

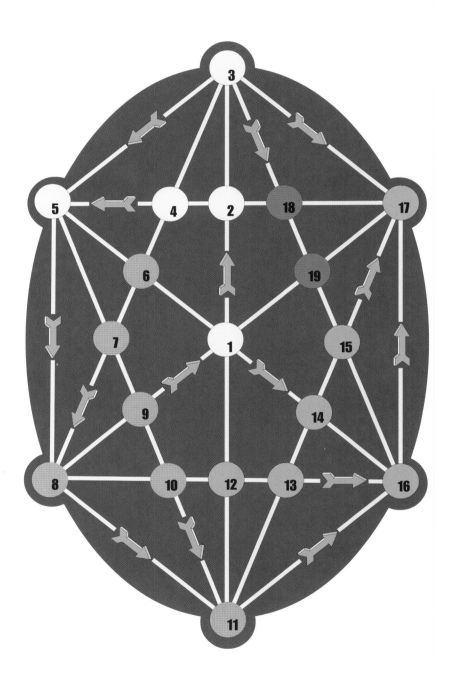

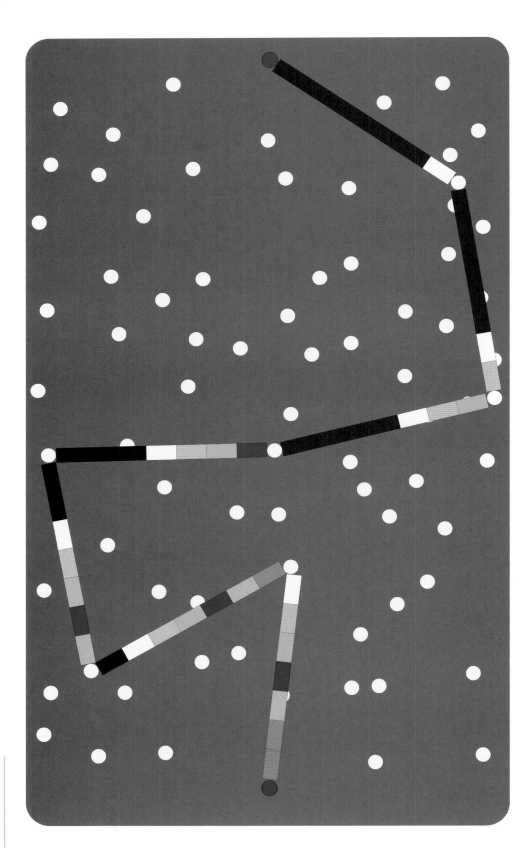

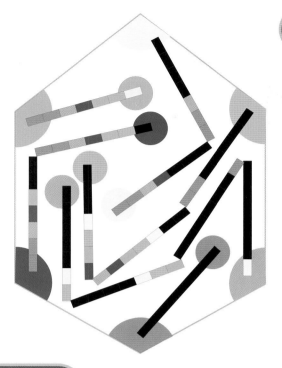

Bin Packing Puzzle

The smallest number of moves needed to achieve the switch is 52.

Icosahedron Route

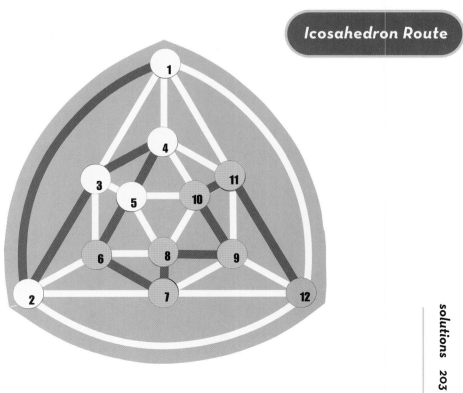

Annihilation

One of the possible solutions.

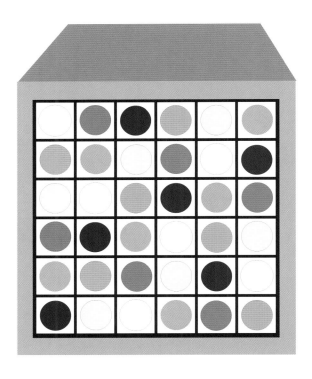

Night Crossing

The other solution: In move 2, hiker 2 crosses back, and hiker 1 crosses on move 4.

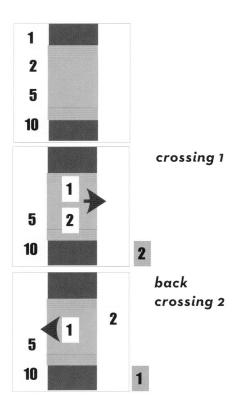

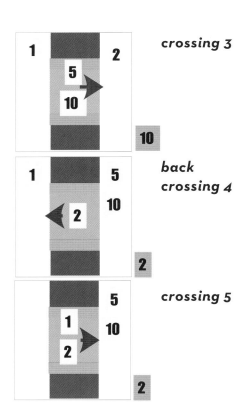

Solitaire Triangles

One possible solution: 6—8, 2—7, 13—4, 15—8, 5—12, 14—5, 1—8, 7—9, 3—8, 11—13, 9—7, 16—8, 7—9, 10—8.

Ganymede Circle

There are five different solutions to the spacings of the six markers, one of which is shown below.

1—2—5—4—6—13
1—2—7—4—12—5
1—3—2—7—8—10
1—3—6—2—5—14
1—7—3—2—4—14

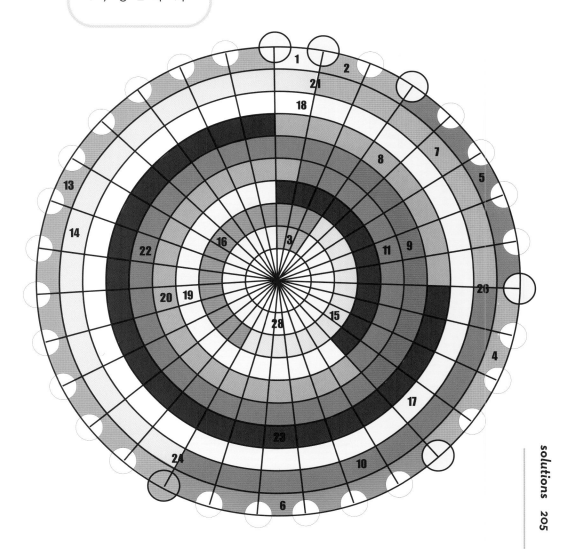

Puzzle 1— One of the many possible solutions with three descending sequences of three numbers and one ascending sequence.
Can you find more?

Puzzle 2— With 10 numbers is would be impossible to avoid either an ascending or descending sequence of four numbers.

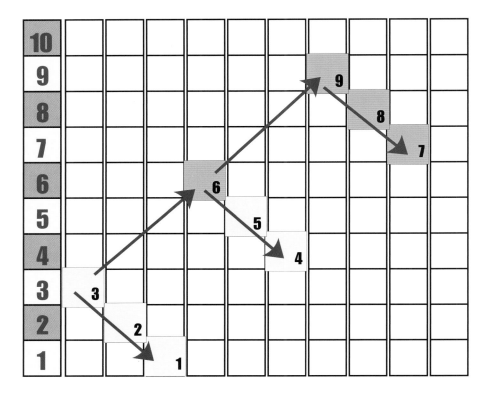

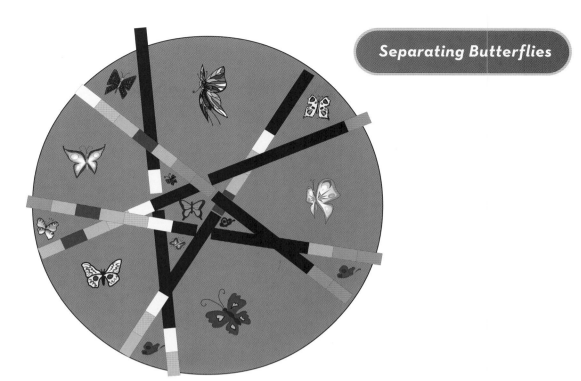

Victor Meally from Ireland found the best solution to Dudeney's puzzle, shown below. It covers a length of 76 field units and visits 63 squares.

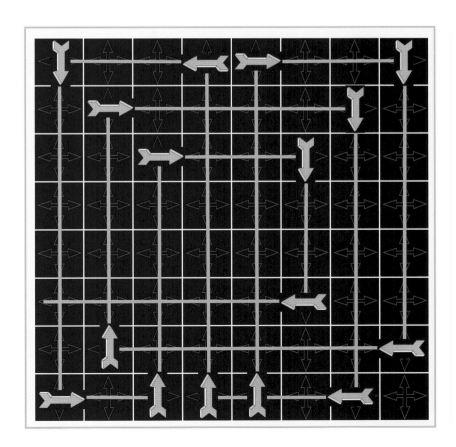

Elevator Trips

It is possible to visit all floors of the building.

The minimum number of journeys to visit all floors is, of course, 19, and the floors will be visited in the following sequence: 0—8—16—5—13—2—10—18—7—15—4—12—1—9—17—6—14—3—11—19. (12 "up" journeys and 7 "down" journeys.)

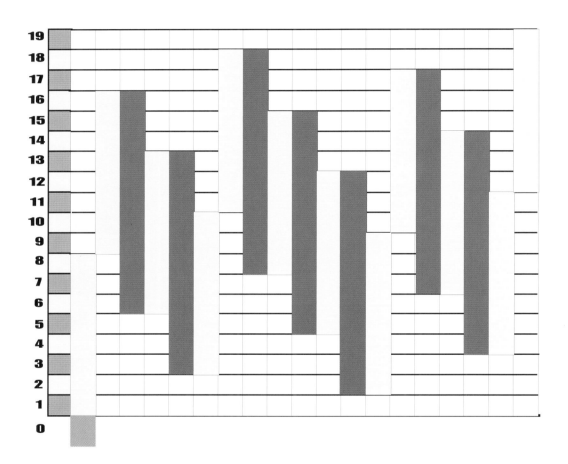

One solution starting from the upper left corner,
visiting all but two cells. Can you do better?

Knights' Exchange

The solution requires 16 moves.

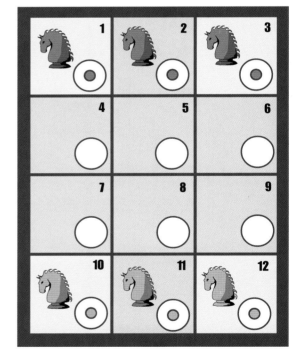

1. 3—4
2. 4—9
3. 11—4
4. 4—3
5. 1—6
6. 6—11
7. 12—7
8. 7—6
9. 6—1
10. 2—7
11. 7—12
12. 9—4
13. 10—9
14. 9—2
15. 4—9
16. 9—10

Peg Solitaire Puzzles

Puzzle 1: 17—15, 28—16, 15—17.
Puzzle 2: 27—25, 25—23, 28—16, 16—4, 4—6, 6—18, 19—17.

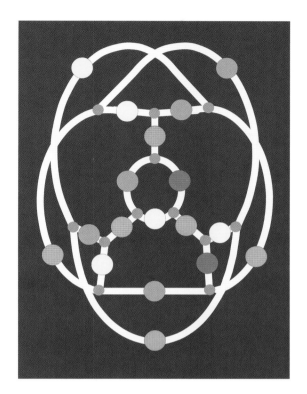

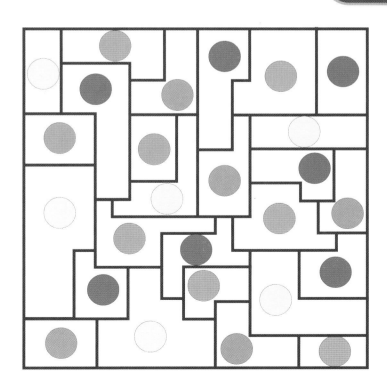

Beads and Necklaces

Here is the set of 18 two-color 7-bead necklaces. It may be of interest to mention that there are 30 necklaces of eight beads; 46 of nine beads; and 78 of ten beads, after which the number of two-color necklaces increases rapidly.

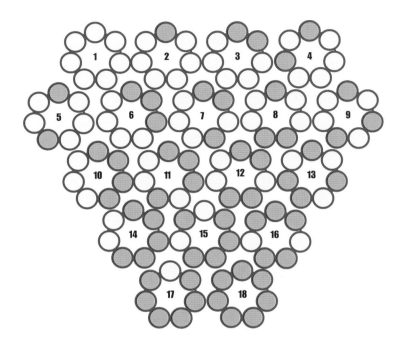

Number Carousel

There are four different solutions, one shown below.

Puzzle 1
Eleven circles. The best packing has two different forms as shown, proven by H. Millissen in 1994.

Puzzle 2
Thirteen circles. The best packing for 13 circles also comes in two different forms. It is interesting to note that one of these is totally rigid, while in the other one there are three loose circles as shown.

　　Both solutions were discovered independently by Kravitz in 1967 and later by Hugo Pfoertner and James Buddenhagen.

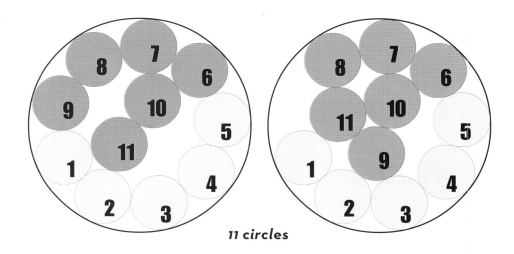

11 circles

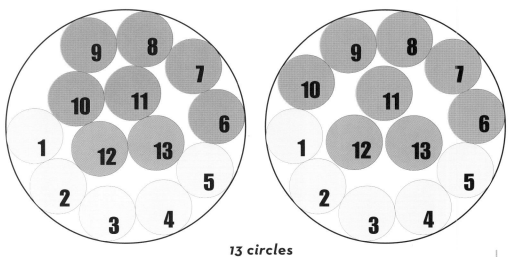

13 circles

Color Dominoes

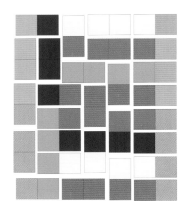 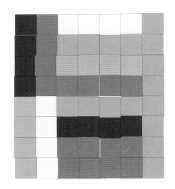 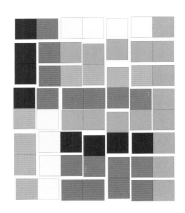

Color Domino Magic Square & Magic Ring

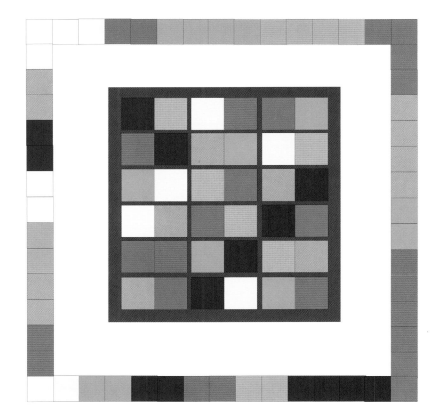

It is believed to be a unique solution.

The general problem for *n* knights: (n–1)(n–2)/2.
Substituting in the eight knights, we get: (8–1)(8–2)/2 = 7 x 6/2 = 21

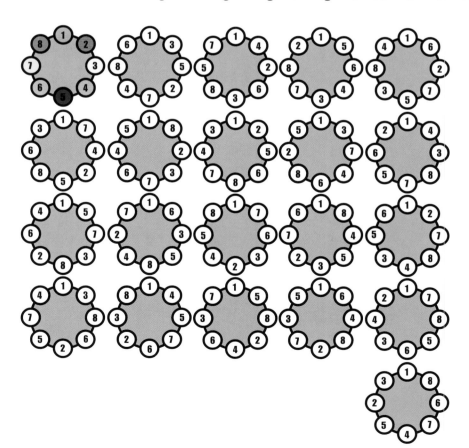

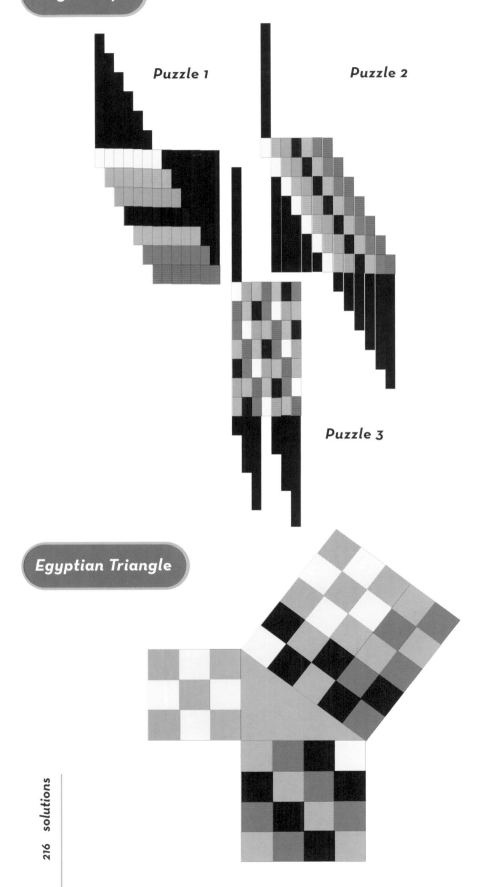

Magic Strips

Puzzle 1

Puzzle 2

Puzzle 3

Egyptian Triangle

Longest Path

A solution in five moves.

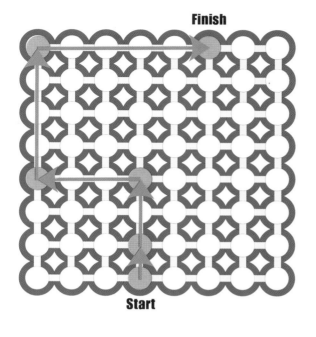

Finish

Start

Packing Circles in Squares

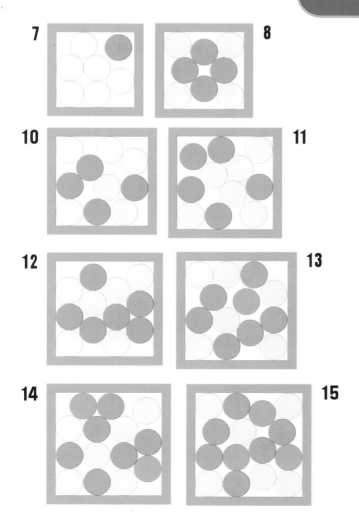

7

8

10

11

12

13

14

15

Railway Puzzle

Nine moves, as shown.

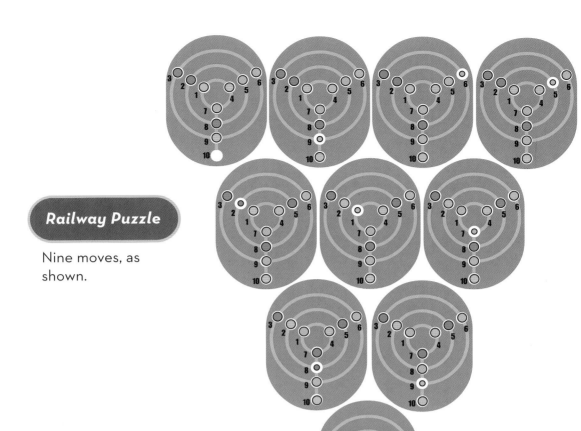

Farrell's Spider

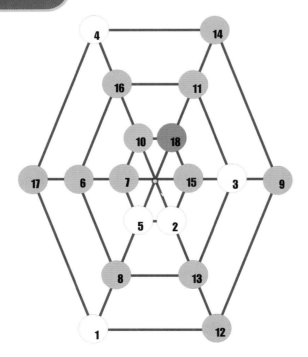

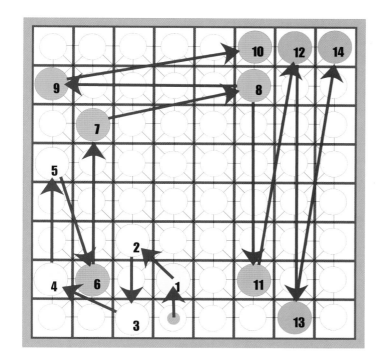

Cellular Paths

14 moves for a square
of side eight.

Man of Law's Puzzle

26 moves:

1	2	3	1	2	6	5	3	1	2	6	5	3	1
2	4	8	7	1	2	4	8	7	4	5	6		

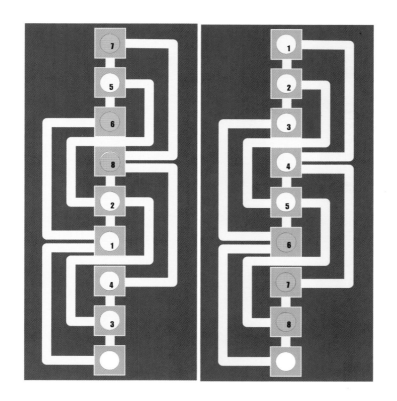

Number Labyrinth

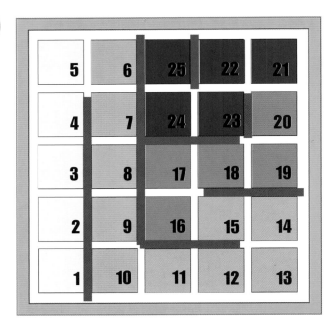

Counter Puzzle

18 moves: 2—3, 9—4, 10—7, 3—8, 4—2, 7—5, 8—6, 5—10, 6—9, 2—5, 1—6, 6—4, 5—3, 10—8, 4—7, 3—2, 8—1, 7—10

Number Neighbors

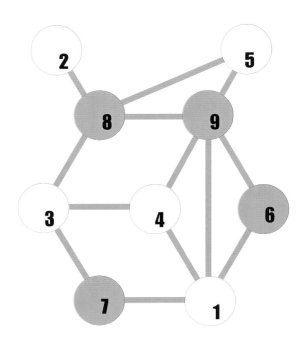

10—5, 1—8, 11—6, 2—9, 12—7, 3—4, 5—12, 8—3, 6—1, 9—10, 7—6, 4—9, 12—7, 3—4, 1—8, 10—5, 6—1, 9—10, 7—2, 4—11, 8—3, 5—12

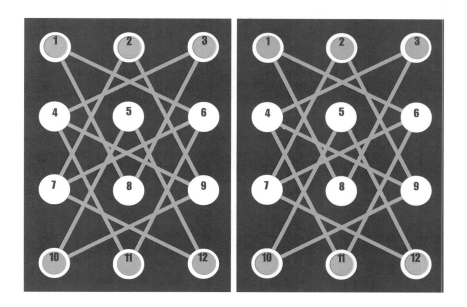

Number Sums and Differences

There are two essentially different solutions:

4	1	5	4	1	3	2	5	3	2
4	5	1	4	3	1	2	3	5	2

Two other solutions can be found by reversing the orders of the sequences.

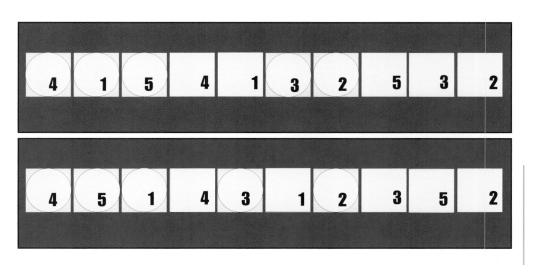

Number Boxes

1	1	2	3	4	5	6
2	7	7	8	9	10	11
3	8	12	12	13	14	15
4	9	13	16	16	17	18
5	10	14	17	19	19	20
6	11	15	18	20	21	21

Four Frogs Switch

1–5, 3–7–1, 8–4–3–7, 6–2–8–4–3, 5–6–2–8, 1–5–6, 7–1

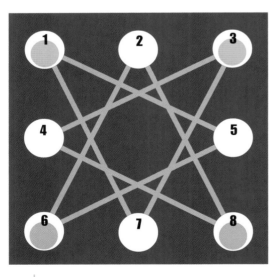 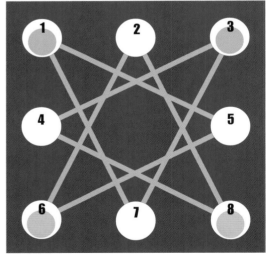

Sixteen weights can be placed in three boxes as shown. Other solutions are possible.

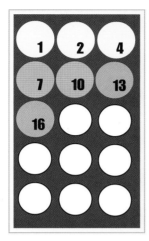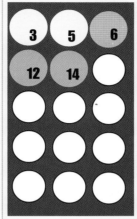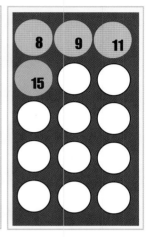

Transformation Switch

The switch can be accomplished in 40 moves:

10L	9R	10R	8L	7L	6L	5L	4L	3L	2L	1L
10U	11U	12U	9U	1R	2R	3D	4D	5U	6U	7U
8U	2U	1L	2L	4U	3L	4L	8R	7R	6D	5L
6L	7L	8L	9L	12R	11R	10				

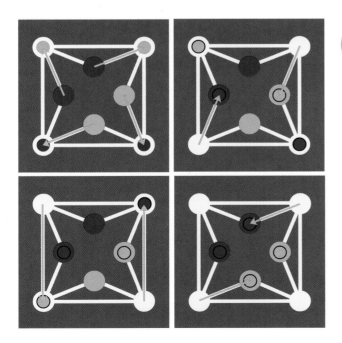

Exchange Moves

Ten moves as shown.

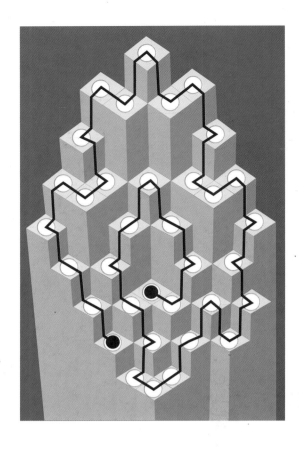

Blocking Roads

The only pathway which makes the puzzle impossible when closed is path 6.

To see why this is impossible, imagine the grid colored checker-board-style, with adjacent circles having different colors (ignoring paths and the symmetric path). You'll see that there are eight white circles and six black circles. If we never use path #6 or the symmetrically equivalent path, every move will alternate from a black circle to a white circle, and it will be impossible to visit every circle. Thus, any path that visits all the circles must do so via path #6.

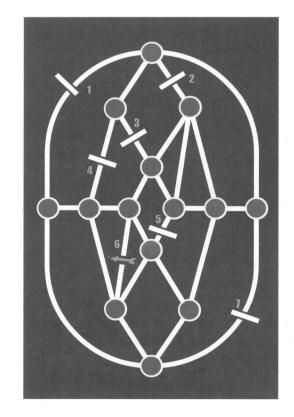